Being Bipolar

Memoirs by M.L. Carmen Forcier

ISBN
978-1-4602-3123-4 (Hardcover)
978-1-4602-3124-1 (Paperback)
978-1-4602-3125-8 (eBook)

Produced by:

FriesenPress

Suite 300 – 852 Fort Street
Victoria, BC, Canada V8W 1H8

www.friesenpress.com

Distributed to the trade by The Ingram Book Company

Let me count the waves

* * *

Trance—Formation

Especially

for Nathan and Phoenix
with so much love…
from your Tu–Tu..

★ ★ ★

My most grateful feelings towards my psychiatrist, Dr. Philip Long
who, with his heart of gold, interest and love,
found the true me, with proper medication
which in turn has given me a peaceful,
healthy and able mind!
With much love and appreciation!
(your favourite girl)

Windows of my soul...
doors to my inner self,
I share with you here
...with open heart.

~M. L. Carmen Forcier~

YOU are a -ONE- derful person
In this UNI (que) VERSE

(Of the NOW time zone)

(Floating between past
And future ETERNITIES)

Through sounds and silences…
ECHOING all the possible possibilities

~ M. L. Carmen Forcier~
Copyright (2008)

T-H-E W-O-R-D

T-o   W-ithin

H-ear   O-urselves,

E-choes   R-eminders,

             D-esires…

At the tender age of thirteen or so, drawn to the magic of television, 'twas
my soul that awakened,
upon hearing the resounding Bostonian voice
of Robert Kennedy, as he quoted
George Bernard Shaw:

Some men see things as they are
and say *why?*
I dream things that never were
and say, *why not?*

My mind blew my heart to new dimensions;
in unison, they vibrated at lightning speed,
Impregnating forever upon my consciousness,
the concept:

ANYTHING IS POSSIBLE!!

NOTE TO MY READERS

You will find theories of my own in the following pages—questions I ask myself—referring at times to what other authors have written, and attempting to blend my thoughts with theirs. I choose to be vulnerable, and am reminded of the phrase:

FAILURE IS NEVER QUITE AS FRIGHTENING AS REGRET.

~Anonymous~

Whatever you can do or dream you can—begin it.
Boldness has genius, power, and magic in it.
Begin it now.

~Goethe~

YOU are my guest. Towards YOU, I extend my Human BEING-NESS, that YOU may feel VALIDATED as a very special person so that you may begin to understand that YOU are PRIORITY NUMBER ONE (for yourself)

May YOU become convinced as to the importance of forgiveness which in fact means giving for yourself.

This conscious effort on my part is to give YOU an opening view of some of my own life experiences, which I feel have caused me to learn lessons, all in the hope that YOU get a glimpse of what is most important to YOU.

As the American motivational speaker LES BROWN says:

"Leap and the net will be there."

This book is my leap of faith (for all people of our planet) ESPECIALLY those of YOU feeling alone, or lonely—those who often feel like giving up, carry low self-esteem or lack self-confidence, believing at times that no one in the world cares for YOU. Please know that over the years, I myself have gone through these very same stages, continually processing whatever needed to be addressed.

"Course correcting," as they say!

In my own words…I say:

It is better to
Love ONE'S SELF
(for a moment)

Than to never have
acknowledged
ONE'S OWN WORTH.

~M. L. Carmen Forcier~
Copyright (1996)

★ ★ ★

WE ARE ALL AWARE OF THE GOLDEN RULE:

DO UNTO OTHERS
AS YOU WOULD HAVE THEM
DO UNTO YOU.

ONE OF MY GOLDEN THOUGHTS SAYS:

DO UNTO YOURSELF
AS YOU WOULD HAVE OTHERS
DO UNTO YOU.

If YOU believe, as I do, that DIVINE SOURCE is pure LOVE and pure LIGHT, and that you are a child of a HIGHER CONSCIOUSNESS, then there is no doubt, my friend, that deep inside, YOU are also pure LOVE and pure LIGHT.

YOU alone make the choice to cultivate your own CONSCIOUSNESS openly, on a daily basis, for your own happiness and peace of mind — always ONE with our eternal galaxies and universes!

Soleil Sourire Sincérité!
~M. L. Carmen Forcier~ © (2003)

I am one drop in the ocean of life,
Swirling, attracting others to see and feel
their own impact on its surface
and in its depth…becoming one
with the shimmering light of the sun…
the flowing of the waves…

~M. L. Carmen Forcier~

INTRODUCTION

Does time assess its own rhythm,
or do our thoughts and memories
arrange themselves
to code time to our individual needs?

~M. L. Carmen Forcier~© (1993)

There are people who suffer from certain chemical imbalances in the brain—people like myself who often experience depression more often and much more deeply than the general population. Many are unaware of this imbalance and often live their whole lives feeling low most of the time, thinking that this is the way life is supposed to feel, because this is all they've known. They've never really hit ROCK BOTTOM or, for that matter, have never reached the possible ten times Heroin HIGH! This is why this illness is still referred to as being manic depressive, meaning the highs and lows.

Others will suffer depression so profoundly that they cannot function well in their daily lives; unless they are properly diagnosed then treated accordingly, they can live very unhappy lives, unable to understand why they are feeling so low, alone and misunderstood.

In many instances, no one actually grasps or questions clearly or even believes in chemical imbalances in the brain!

Just as a diabetic person needs insulin, a mentally challenged person needs medication to stabilize the brain's unseen waves of activities. If it is a case of a chemical imbalance where one is truly unable to stop this process of feeling so down and out or feeling very high, then the person in question needs to acknowledge that they really need to seek professional help. Often, an accurate diagnosis is difficult to determine, as some illnesses resemble one another very closely.

For example, I'm somewhat aware that schizophrenia and manic-depression (known today as Bipolar) are somewhat linked. I say this because of my own personal experience of having been misdiagnosed as schizophrenic at age twenty-five. For one full year, I took meds for schizophrenia!

In 1980 I was finally correctly diagnosed as having BIPOLAR ONE illness at the age of twenty-six. This brings back memories of how my mind would go beyond the reality that most people live within.

Bipolar illness (when you're HIGH) takes you into dimensions that are hardly explainable; even physicians who are trained to assist the mentally challenged will never truly comprehend the inner world of this illness unless they personally experience them. Yes, they've studied the symptoms and possible combination of meds to help alleviate the suffering of their patients.

At the same time, speaking only for myself, I've sometimes asked my own psychiatrist why he would not want to know the details of my so-called highs or trips.

His response is that it is not useful to understand what the mind tears through, while in this HIGH state. Medically speaking, psychiatrists focus more on bringing the patient back down to normalcy with medication.

ON BEING

Shakespeare wrote,

TO BE OR NOT TO BE,
that is the question.

Can it also be an answer?

In other words,
I AM or I AM NOT
AM I or AM I NOT?
Can be interpreted as meaning:

"I am this kind of person and not any other kind of person"
sounds too simplistic.
Let's think instead that one moment we are conscious
and the next moment
we metaphorically fall asleep—
for the mind wanders
and wonders through time…
RE-membering, RE-living, RE-miniscing
then RE-surfacing to the present
where we notice we are back in the NOW time zone,
only to continue this pattern of going back to memories
—coming forth again
into the present consciousness of feeling alive.

As our thoughts sway between the windows
of feeling alive or feeling asleep,

we can conclude
that at times,
WE ARE
and at times,
WE ARE NOT (conscious).

Therefore, to live in the moment, for me,
is a feeling that I've personally been experiencing
since I was fifty-four;
inhaling time into shorter bits of reality
in an attempt to breathe more easily.
Instead of taking life one day at a time, I separate them into one hour segments.

The word *wonder* is to ponder or think of something or someone, to be in
wonder
of a person, place or thing...to feel, imagine
or contemplate being wonder–full
and noticing this wonder–fullness in others
as well as in our immediate surroundings.
To be full of wonder is also temporary,
for the mind continues its course of being
aware,
unaware,
flowing back and forth
from one dimension to the other.
Sometimes we harmonize with life
and then, if we become worried or upset,
we feel disconnected or unhappy...
(though we are still alive in the same manner)

The harmony we felt just moments ago,
is still there; simply said.
When we choose to change our thought patterns to fear,
we feel we are no longer connected
to the DIVINE SOURCE.

Whatever this means to you:
Whether it be
INFINITE WISDOM
YOUR INNER STRENGTH,
POWER OF YOUR SOUL,
LOVE
or
YOUR CREATIVE IMAGINATION…
I believe that the SOURCE is the same for all of creation; we
are always connected to this SOURCE—though at times we
do not sense it, as the SOURCE never ceases to exist.

We simply, by way of nature, go through stages of growth
when we feel detached from the wonder of life
in order to learn clarity
from the lessons we are meant to understand.

At a certain age, we become aware
that life is the same
as the ebb and flow of the waters.
Back and forth, our thoughts are pleasant or unpleasant,
whether we NOTE-ice them or not.

To keep our feelings balanced,
we must condition ourselves to Re-mind our heart
that pain is not a permanent stage of being
and that we will again and again return
to the harmony felt so many other times before.
When we are down we tend to forget
that we will again float back up…to feel better!

May you be reminded here of what Helen Keller once said:

ALTHOUGH THE WORLD IS FULL OF SUFFERRING,
IT IS ALSO FULL OF THE OVERCOMING OF IT.

Thus, our lives are filled with ups and downs
as a roller-coaster ride.

Ride the wave, as the saying goes.
This is probably where the word FAITH comes into play,
knowing that pain means growth
and that there is always something to learn.

Personally, when my tide is low, my brain asks,
What is the lesson here?
What am I supposed to better understand?
in order to become a more compassionate person?

So herein lies my mini interpretation of
TO BE OR NOT TO BE.

Whether it is a question seeking an answer
or an answer to a question,
YOU choose!

When I touch one note
of the songs people carry in their hearts,
the love for the children within us all
will continue to broaden
into a brotherhood of all men

~M. L. Carmen Forcier~
Copyright (1995)

PART ONE

DISTURBING
DYNAMICS

MY BIRTHPLACE

What this power is I cannot say;
all I know is that it exists.

~Alexander Graham Bell~

Born in Windsor, Ontario, Canada, I inhaled my very first breath of life on a Saturday morning at 7:20 am, October, 4, 1954. Although I am a bilingual French-Canadian, I was named Marie Liliane Carmen Frappier; "Carmen" is Spanish for 'song'; it's also a Greek word.

I was the first child to my parents, who were then considered to have married late in life, having said, "I DO" on October 24, 1953—at which time my mom was thirty-two, and my dad forty-one.

There I was, with such a full head of very dark hair that my mom, upon arriving home, quickly took her hairdressing scissors and cut off most of this full mane of mine. She has repeated over time how much I looked like a little monkey. My father's words, over many years, would often remind me of how ugly I looked when he first set eyes on me—in his own words, he compared me to an ugly baby monkey!

As soon as I was old enough to understand these thoughts, they began slowly but surely to destroy my self-esteem. Still, from what one of my mom's sisters told me in my teens, my parents were absolutely overwhelmed at having me as their child, especially at their age!

The real shock would come two years down the road when my personality began emerging. My imagination and enthusiasm were a little bit much for two people who had lived relatively quiet lives during their single years—plus, they had baggage of their own, which in those days was not spoken of, only because they never even knew what baggage was in the first place!

As my mom and dad told the story, for one week following my birth, I kept vomiting in a projectile manner. They waited for the weekend to pass—then, on Monday morning, October 13, my father finally phoned the paediatrician to explain my situation; the physician immediately prescribed a tablespoon of a certain liquid to be taken at each meal, helping my digestive tract. My dad started giving me this tablespoon of medicine, following the proper dosage, and sure enough, my system was able to take in the milk formula without getting sick, although another problem occurred.

That evening, quite late, I kept crying. My dad (mentally incapable of hearing a child cry) had come into my room to hold a soother to my mouth, though to no avail. He then noticed I felt hot to touch and did not have a clue as to what to do. Thinking quickly, he ran to the neighbour's house and asked Mrs. Quenville (whom he knew well) to come straight over. Luckily she knew how to take a baby's temperature. Three minute later and there it was—my temperature was 104 degrees (Fahrenheit)!

Well, talk about rushing to the hospital; both my parents were frantic! My dad drove as fast and as carefully as possible while my mom held me in her arms.

Upon arriving at the hospital, doctors examined me, said I'd been poisoned, and that my chances of survival were nil! Totally bewildered and beside themselves, my parents were dumbfounded! How could this be? She was doing fine after the medicine! THE MEDICINE!

"Oh," the doctors said, "how much has she been taking?"

In intensive care, I was under constant observation while my parents waited in the hallway, filled with grief, shock and disbelief! I was the first child of this elderly couple. Would they ever be blessed with another?

How could my paediatrician have prescribed this apparently high dose of medication to such a small infant? As these and many other questions swam through their minds, a nun came to sit quietly beside my mom.

As the question was asked, "Is she going to be OK?" the nun shook her head, said she was very sorry, but NO, the child, me, would not live!

My mom's thoughts were that if God wanted to take me, then she willingly accepted this sudden tear in her heart. I actually spent the night at the hospital, recovering. The next day I was discharged. That was my first close encounter with death. Unbeknownst to anyone, there were to be more!

As it turned out, one tablespoon was too much for my little body. From then on, I would be given one *teaspoon* of this medicine, every couple of hours.

★ ★ ★

Later on in my life, I heard a true story about a baby who weighed approximately two pounds—incubated with intravenous lines every which way—who would go into cardiac arrest and seizures a little too often, it seemed. After saving the baby's heart for the umpteenth time, and as the last nurse started turning away, the child went into cardiac arrest once again. Now, this was a very big mystery to all concerned as he was doing this way too often, statistically speaking, if you will.

This particular nurse had an idea. She took an intravenous pole, brought it as near to the child's head and eyes as possible, drew a face on the intravenous bag, then wrapped a large yellow gown around the IV pole.

That baby, according to the reliable sources I'd heard from, never had another attack of any kind. Why, you may ask? Well, according to the ICU staff on shifts with this child, it was concluded that this baby could see shadows and was apparently reassured by the disguised IV pole possibly believing it was a REAL person—go figure, eh?

Thus, in closing, this first episode of my life, I have remained the child who constantly has to be followed up by some type of medical specialist. May it be said that there remains a great comfort and companionship between all of the white coats and myself whenever I see a doctor.

As a BIPOLAR person, being the centre of attention (personally speaking) is very much needed and craved!

Validation...Validation...
The prayer...we all seek!

~M.L. Carmen Forcier~
(Copyright 2003)

JANUARY—FEBRUARY, 1954

If there is any peace,
it will come through being, not knowing.

~Henry Miller~

My aunt Lilianne, sister to my mom, had been in a convent in Montréal, Québec, Canada, for a while. She begged my grand-parents to come to a ceremony where she would be taking her vows (or something to this nature). Mémé and Pépé asked my parents as well as my uncle Léo, (my mom's brother) if they would drive from Windsor, Ontario to Montréal, Québec, for this special occasion, as they felt incapable of making the trip themselves.

Upon leaving the convent, after all of the congratulations, it was beginning to snow. By morning, they awoke to see a storm had caused the roads to be covered in black ice.

My uncle Léo felt more confident driving than my dad…so there they were, slipping and sliding, in a very dangerous situation. By the time they arrived in Windsor, my mom (who'd always tired in the car) felt quite sick; she was vomiting, feeling weak, etc. My dad immediately drove her to the hospital.

A few tests later, the doctor said: "You're pregnant."

My mother shared this story with me in May of 2008 (at age 87)

She said: "I knew nothing! I thought I was too old to have children. I didn't even know how babies were conceived or born!"

She also added here that she'd been x-rayed when she was four months pregnant with me (this alone may have caused my unhealthy challenges over time). And so, nine months passed, and there I was, this child, this miracle.

My earliest memory is one where my mom is sitting me pretty; then, a big bright light flashes in my face. Believe it or not, that flash was from the camera of a professional photographer and I was only ONE YEAR OLD!

★ ★ ★

My parents, over the years, took pictures like it was going out of style! The most painful moment of my early life occurred at the age of two. My mom, holding a camera, said to me, most impatiently: "Look at your baby!!"

The only recollection I have of that moment was that my mom had put something in MY doll's carriage, and that this had upset me very much! As she took the picture, sure, my head was facing that something in the carriage; I fooled her by closing my eyes tightly, as I could not bear to see what was replacing my dolls.

The memory I have of noticing my sister for the first time is when my dad came home from work one day; I'd just stepped on her tiny hand while she'd been crawling. She was approximately a year old. My father picked her up immediately, and YELLED at me for being so careless.

My response was that I had not done it on purpose (I would use this sentence throughout my life). That memory was most hurtful for little me! Why?

The little queen I'd been, for both my parents, was no longer a reality. I'd lost my place, became less important in their eyes and have never had a close relationship with my sister to this day! This was my experience in seeing and feeling my dad's violent temper towards my inner child.

As my sister and I grew up, my father would spend HOURS (over time) yelling at me, often calling me the Satanic child because I did not like to play with my sister. He had to scream his head off!

I still remember seeing his thin, balding hair flying out from his head. Knowing this was a sign of great danger, I'd force myself to play with her, something I absolutely loathed.

My mother always tells me that after my sister was born, I never held another doll. They must have reminded me that my life as the little queen had been permanently taken away. My sister now held the place of honour!

For myself, I tend to think that as a BIPOLAR person, this was very devastating to me. I simply LOVE and sometimes really NEED to be the centre of attention at all times!

In the final analysis, we are left alone with only ourselves, to ponder on what we have given and what we have taken.

~Oprah Show~

This may be why I remember most of my living moments, from being one year old and onward. I was so FULL OF LIFE! I was very expressive with lots of enthusiasm. This was very hard on my parents as they were ready to slow down and almost semi-retire!

I'd force myself to play house with my sister; that's pretty much all she wanted to do. I disliked this immensely, feeling that I was wasting my time when I could have been playing a game, colouring or playing outside with my little friends.

My mom was thirty-three years old when she had me, and my dad was forty-two! My sister Gizèle was born two years following my birth. When my mom turned thirty-eight, she miscarried.

My father came home early that day, took my little cardboard suitcase (which I still have) from my closet and said we were going to Mémé and Pépé's for a while. My sister was almost three and I was nearing my fifth birthday. Then my father told us to go say good-bye to maman, as she would be away for a while.

Of course, we had no clue as to what was happening. Taking my sister's hand (I felt protective of her in moments of sadness), we walked into my parent's room; maman was crying so hard that it was very painful and very scary to hear her, as she TRIED to tell us to be good for her parents. We were then taken out of her room as the AMBULANCE had arrived with a stretcher.

I'd seen on TV when they would cover a person's head with a white sheet, it meant that person was dead. Well, once they neared the front door to wheel my mom away, the attendants covered her head with a white sheet! You can only imagine my total shock!

My father was talking to one of our neighbours out on the front lawn and now, in retrospect, he was saying that she'd lost the baby. He looked pretty shaken, feeling helpless, and probably very disappointed they'd lost a child.

Years later, we found out that my mom, that day, had been hemorhaging quite heavily; the foetus had been exposed to either red or German measles which my sister had contracted.

MY FATHER...

...For the skylight is like skin
and all the rain falls down...Amen.

~Leonard Cohen~

Once my sister was born, my father chose to prefer her over me, thus, setting me aside. He was ALWAYS blaming me for anything and everything that would happen between me and her. Another thing that made him angry was that I was not perfect enough. He was "THE" perfectionist.

Looking back today, my sister and I, both being Registered Nursing Assistants (having graduated in the province of Ontario, Canada), truly believe that our mom had Postpartum Depression after my birth, never having received treatment of any kind at any time. One reason we can rely on this theory is that one of my mom's sisters was diagnosed with manic depression (better known today as BIPOLAR illness) when she was approximately forty-nine years of age. When this occurred, my father's brain was awakened; he explained to my sister that my mom had totally changed after giving birth to me.

He apparently had finally put two and two together, and by remembering my aunt's behaviour over the years, said my mom had the same characteristics. My aunt has been seeing a psychiatrist since her diagnosis, although she's never been very well-balanced on her medication; AND my mom has ALWAYS been a harsh, angry, bitter and unhappy person, at times a little high, especially when getting ready for church—possible signs of either BIPOLAR TWO or UNIPOLAR (meaning depression)?

My mom's religion has kept her in the dark, alienated from most people, depressed and terribly angry with the world, etc. For example, when one of my uncles passed away, she declared he was in purgatory. He had not followed the word of the Lord nor had he ever attended mass. SHE was always passing judgment on everyone!

★ ★ ★

The result today is that my mom, having turned ninety two years of age April of 2013, has a very unattractive character, hates most everything and everyone. My heart goes out to her because "if people knew better they would do better"

(This is one of my own quotes)

She wasn't the type to go out and have coffee with someone although she had a good friend, my aunt Lucie, and of course all of the other women who came to get their hair done every week.

My sister and I believe that she may be UNIPOLAR as she lives in a very dark, depressing space. Or, she may have BIPOLAR TWO which is where a patient never experiences the HIGHS, only the lows. (Bipolar ONE means you have highs and lows.)

She has NEVER been medically treated nor has she ever been seen by any kind of professional in regards to this subject. My dad just let it all ride!

While I was growing up, my father had given up on my mom, as she never wanted to discuss ANYTHING with him. At one point, my sister and I knew there was no sexual relationship between them. Anger reigned in the house almost every Sunday morning, to the point where my dad would scream and scream at my mom. This chaos mounted with more and more tension over the years, which resulted in my father pouting in one corner, my mom screaming in the other! It was hell on earth!

Living with my grand-parents most of the time as a toddler may not have been only because of my father's temper, but also due to my mother's swinging moods, THEN and NOW!

PLUS…my sister and I never really got along with each other. One of the main reasons why she and I were always fighting like leopards was very much due to the fact that my dad did not want us to get along. This satisfied some of his own inner anger and it actually pleased him every time my sister told on me because he'd defend her on any subject whereas I NEVER behaved well enough to meet his standards. I learned at a very young age to try to defend myself against him and spent most of his living days disagreeing with his gruelling character.

My sister always prayed I would not fight back but I always did; I had learned the anger game and would learn from a very early age to fight all my life, to make things fair for myself and others! I REALLY WANTED TO BE RIGHT!

Yes, I realize as the saying goes, "You inherit half of your mother's genes and half of your father's," although I came across a quote that said it a little differently; at a certain age we all come to a point in our lives when we choose who we want to become!

My angry behaviour could have been related to being BIPOLAR. In later years, my psychiatrist often said that science does not know if a patient born with this particular illness can be more seriously ill if the patient comes from a broken home. I believe I'm one of those whose illness was made worse due to my deplorable upbringing!

ATTENTION FROM MY MOM…

One must grieve in order to leave the past behind.

~M.L. Carmen Forcier~

Attention from my mom was very much needed on my part, many times. Some mornings, while getting ready for school, I'd wait for a disturbing feeling to occur in my stomach; then, knowing I was telling the truth, I'd let my mom know that I felt too sick to go to school.

She'd then say: "Well, then get back into bed."

I think I spent most of my time reading, and every time I stayed home with my fake illness, my mom would bring me tomato soup TO MY BED! Now that felt like love!

There was one drawback of course, one that my father came up with: if we had not gone to school on a certain day, we could not play outside nor inside with our friends that same evening.

I once got up enough nerve to ask my dad, on one of those days: "Could I please play outside? I'm feeling so much better"

…and his answer …would be?

BRIEF NOTES

On many occasions, my dad would approach my mom and say that he wanted her to know their finances in case he died before her. She always sent him on his way, stating that she was not interested in what he had to say; she would figure it out, once he passed on.

My sister once shared with me her experience the 1st day I attended kindergarten. My mom, an at-home hairdresser, closed the door of the den in my sister s face, meaning, "Go play with your dolls, find something to do, because I'm too busy!"

My sister felt so rejected, unable to respond either by crying or complaining, as these reactions were never tolerated in our house!

★ ★ ★

Ever since I can remember, my sister always had watery eyes. Later on, I was to learn that this can be the cause of a repressed emotional life.

FOND MEMORIES...

A problem is a chance to do your best.

~Duke Ellington~

Fond memories of my maternal grand-parents inspired me to write this simple poem!

My Mémé and Pépé

As a child so delighted
And so often excited
To see my Mémé
And Pépé come take me

To their home I did go
Hearing the piano
I was to inherit
When afford could my parents

My Pépé would greet me
With a grasp in the air
Hold me, uplift me
With such loving care

My Pépé was gifted
With knowledge of wood
And once made a chair

That hold I could
In my three-year-old hand
To this day it still stands

My Mémé would cook
I'd watch her and then
We'd eat at the table
A most quiet moment

Until Pépé would say
"Is there no tea, Mémé?
I'm choking, I'm choking.
Bring the tea—hurry!"
(of course he was joking)

My Mémé for sure
Always had ready
A pot full of tea
For my dear Pépé

When it was time
We'd get in the car
On the seat I would stand
Mémé's hand as my guard

Pépé took walks
Smoking cigars
While Mémé and me
Pushed a grocery cart

Mémé would hold
An item in hand
Thinking and looking
Down the aisle and beyond

Sometimes she'd place it
Into the basket
And other times the item
Went back where she'd found it

M. L. CARMEN FORCIER

At times she'd hesitate
Her arm on the shelf
Then swiftly the treat
Found itself
Alongside her other
Purchases like butter, ketchup and mustard

My Pépé would help
Put the food in the trunk
And then we'd be off
The groceries were done.

Standing in the middle
Of the seat once again
Apparently when little
I'd say, "Maison à Canne!"
Recognizing my street
While in Pépé's Buick.

After eating a meal
And Pépé's tea served
Mémé would ask me
Did I want dessert?

Only she'd say it
With cookies in hand
The treat she'd hesitated with
Then quickly taken

She'd say, "Want a cookie?"
I could not say no,
For I knew what my Mémé
Had been through to show

Her love for me when
Her pennies were few
I cry to this day
"Mémé Thank you"

I miss my Mémé
And Pépé so much
And wish they were here
To comfort and touch.

Always remember
A kindness from someone
Especially from those
Whose love for you once

Was so full and eternal,
You knew not its full power...

~M. L. Carmen Forcier
~ (© 2003)

TERRIFYING TIMES
TROUBLING TEARS

AT ONE POINT…

*The secret to life
is enjoying the passage of time.*

~James Taylor~

My mom had let me out of my playpen; it was wonderful to roam around—
I felt so free! Then, one day, she wanted to vacuum the house, so she put
me back in the surrounded play area so that I would not be in her way.
Well, talk about feeling locked up! I screamed and screamed, out of terror,
horrified by the sound of this machine!!

My very first childhood friends, at the age of 3, were called Peter, Joey,
Pat, Patricia and Tony. At about the same time, my parents had bought me
a role-away bed and they'd also given me a pillow! This was a big event
for me.

One day, shortly thereafter, while sitting on our porch steps, Patricia, who
was about 10 years of age, came to sit with me. I was so excited that I said
she could use my new bed anytime, especially my pillow!

On another occasion my little friend Tony, asked if I would go with him to
see this old lady. We were about 4 or 5 at the time. So about 4 doors down
from my house, Tony and I came face to face with this crabby old woman
sitting on her porch. She was an angry S.O.B.!

She asked us if we would go to the corner store to buy her a pop-sicle. She gave us a nickel and we did what she asked, only on our way back, Tony said to me... To heck with her, let s split this for the 2 of us!

When we got in front of her home, she was furious!!! She could see that we were both enjoying the treat she had paid for!! She got up from her rocking chair, leaning over the fenced porch, livid with anger because we had tricked her. She was fuming!!

All of a sudden, because she's leaning so far into the ledge, she tumbles, head first, rolling over and falls into the big bush just below her. Man we were scared!!

A woman and young man ran out of the house to see what was going on. Tony and I just stood there in shock, saying we were very sorry!

The young woman said it was OK-- that her mother often went into fits of rage and that it was not our fault. We were free to go!

(That blue pop-sicle was deliciously refreshing in Windsor's high humidity heat!)

P.S.

My parents had one of my grandmother's uncles, Napoléon Cadieux, renting the room at the back of our house. He always ate dinner with us and had a way of making my sister and I laugh to ourselves whenever he took a gulp from his glass of milk. You see, he would let the white mustache stay on the top of his lips, pretending as if nothing and every single night we would have a good quiet laugh about this because we truly believed that he had no idea why we were giggling. No one ever mentioned the subject out loud!

After dinner he would get his coat and scarf - - wishing us a good evening while he went for a long walk. Oftentimes, I would hear my dad and him playing cribbage late at night, pounding their fists on the kitchen table when they scored. Fond memories of this uncle remain today.

LITTLE JOEY...

Friendship is a single soul dwelling in two bodies.

~Aristotle~

...as your friend, I am with you, spiritually—at all times.

~Carmen~

Little Joey turned out to be Gizèle's first boyfriend; he'd even given her a small ring. They would go for walks with his mom and she often treated them to candies.

One morning, as I was leaving for school, Ena, Joey's mom, came to ask my mom if she could take my sister to the store. My mom said yes. Now, because I was SO powerfully jealous of my sister, with her being the favoured child and having all the fun while I had to go to school, it often felt like I was being punished, and that hurt me a lot!

At the age of six, walking out the door, I opened my big mouth and loudly said to Ena: "My mom said Gizèle cannot go with you."

This gave me great satisfaction and kind of evened out the privileges that my sister always received. I was not getting the love or attention for which I so starved! I was highly angry. This type of reaction/behaviour can, at times, be seen in people with Bipolar illness!

★ ★ ★

My mom would often set us up in our small blown-up pool in the backyard so that she could concentrate her time on hairdressing. Now, I was really afraid to touch grass with my feet as I'd seen my mom clean the tub after our baths; once, seeing her pick up a gob of hair from the drain gave me the creeps and caused me to transfer that fear to the icky feeling of walking on the grass, as if I were walking on big gobs of hair. So when my sister and I had played long enough in the water, on every occasion, I would sit in the pool, alone, calling my mom to come get me across the grass.

She would finally appear, yelling her head off, repeating she had no time for this, and could I just smarten up and get out of the darn pool?

MY FIRST HALLOWEEN...

*To live heroically is its own compensation in which
all can share. In every person, there's a slumbering hero.*

~Henry Neumann~

I remember my first Halloween experience: at age three, I'd seen masks looking into our home through the front door, and I screamed as if someone was going to kill me. This kind of dramatization can at times be seen in people with BIPOLAR illness. How was I to know that these were only masks and not true faces of real people?

The following year, my mom took me out to trick or treat. It was a very nice experience, because behind every door, someone gave me candies, peanuts and chocolate bars!

My mom, always being very concerned about our teeth, would make these candies last for a year or more, hiding them high enough in the kitchen cupboards, totally preventing us from sneaking any of these goodies.

Around this same age, I would often notice the milkman when he came to deliver at our door, his cargo being pulled by a nice medium brown horse, whose eyes were covered by blinkers. Being of curious mind, I approached the horse by taking a few steps on the small sidewalk nearing the curb, which I knew was forbidden territory, as it was very close to the street.

I took my chances and gently leaned forward to try and see the horse's eyes, as I wanted to know if he was sad. At that very moment, my father's watchful eye caught me standing where I'd been told not to go. He raised his voice, yelling out: "Carmen, get out of there!"

No surprise to me!! I simply felt sad for the horse as he seemed so alone.

★ ★ ★

One day, my aunt Lilianne was visiting, dressed as a nurse. She was the one I admired the most because she was so pretty and funny. I was just over three years old, and she'd made such an impression on me that I promised myself I would also one day become a nurse.

WHEN MY SISTER GIZELE...

*There are few joys that rival being outside
on a beautiful day in the company of a good book.*

~Oprah Winfrey~

When my sister Gizele was two and I was four years of age, we were in the habit of placing chewing gum on the radio shelf in the kitchen; we always chewed it for at least a week before it would fall apart.

One day, my mother was out and my sister asked my father if she could have a new piece of gum. He reached high up into the cupboard and gave her a fresh piece. As he did so, I dared ask for one for myself, as my own gum had dried into a few un-chewable pieces.

My father was SO enraged that he angrily screamed at me: "Carmen, don't you lie to me!"

I quickly explained myself, but his look was one of pure disgust. He finally handed me a new piece, frightening me to the point where I thought I'd go to jail!

★ ★ ★

My mom always put us to bed at7 pm as she had read somewhere that a child needed twelve hours of sleep in order to be well-rested. Well, needless to say, I could never fall asleep. I was the type of child who would easily get excited about life in general and had a hard time winding down. (This can occur in people with BIPOLAR illness.)

Later on in my life, I would learn that the first question a psychiatrist asks his bipolar patients is, "How many hours of sleep are you getting?" You see, it is possible that because I was BIPOLAR (remembering that some of us are apparently born with chemical imbalances), not sleeping enough over a certain period of time can cause a HIGH.

★ ★ ★

Late one night, at the age of four, I walked from my bed to the living room, seeing my father rocking my sleeping sister in his arms. I asked him if he could rock ME to sleep.

He mocked me in a disgusting sharp voice by saying: "You're too old for this; go back to bed!"

My heart broke wide open.

BRIEF NOTES

My parents called me by name mostly when they were angry. As French was always spoken in the home, it took me until I was the age of thirty-five to accept anyone calling me by name in French without feeling I was being punished.

★ ★ ★

One day, after school, I was surprised to see my mom picking me up with a strange man at the steering wheel. She asked me if I remembered my uncle Reginald (one of my dad's brothers). I wanted to be honest and said, "No."

Upon approaching home, there was my paternal grandfather, standing on the sidewalk, anticipating my arrival. Him, I remembered! They'd driven from Sudbury, Ontario, all in one day, so they must have been pretty tired!

M. L. CARMEN FORCIER

Pépé had always squeezed my sister and I very close to him; this was his way of showing his love, being so deaf.

★ ★ ★

My dad came from a small village in northern Ontario called Sturgeon Falls. My mother also came from up north, in the same province, not too far away from there, in another small town called Noelville. The interesting thing is that they met each other in Windsor, Ontario many years later!

Authentic spirituality awakens the soul,
Reconnects us with the sacred,
and fills us with the passion of life.
Spiritual development is not about religious rituals and practices,
It is about waking up to the wonder of life.

~David N. Elkins~

BEING A GOOD PARENT…

The sky is the daily bread of the eyes.

~Ralph Waldo Emerson~

Being a good parent is an art unto itself. Even though my father had a bad temper, he would somewhat soften up once in a while.

My mother was distant and never really knew how to talk to us. There was also very little communication between her and my father. In the very early years of our lives, after a long day's work, my father would sometimes kneel on the floor then tickle us till we had to beg him to stop.

Those moments were happy and rare. As for my mom, she lost our respect over the years, as we were always sinning by disobeying.

Every day since I was two, I was told I was going to "…burn in HELL—FOREVER—for all of ETERNITY!" if I disobeyed my parents or anyone else!

Also, growing up, Sundays were so depressing with church and confessions. It took me about eight years after I was married (at the age of twenty-six) to finally start loving Sundays!

★ ★ ★

It was easier for my parents to raise us as little ones. As we grew into our teens, they lost their grip and everything went haywire!

* * *

My sister and I never wore pants till we were twelve and ten.

We'd worn dresses and skirts all of our lives. This was a very strict rule in our house!

M. L. CARMEN FORCIER

MY FIRST SCHOOL…

There is not a single true work of art that has not in the end added to the inner freedom of each person who has known and loved it.

~Albert Camus~

….was called St. Edmonds where I attended kindergarten and grade one. This school of mine taught all French classes, up to the eighth grade. At the end of grade one, the nun I'd had as a teacher, Sister Louise Marie, took me downstairs to say good-bye to my kindergarten teacher. I could not even speak. Mme Marteleau was told I was moving away and not coming back to this school

BRIEF NOTE

Years later in (1964)…when I was 10 and in 5th grade…there was a French concert at the brand new school of St. Edmond's. My mom took my sister and I to see the plays and to hear the students' choir, all in French! It was fantastic!

Afterwards, I started roaming the hallways looking for Mme Marteleau. Now, I hardly looked like I did when I was 6 years old! I enter this class-room where there's this woman erasing the blackboard. I recognize her right away and say, Mme Marteleau, do you remember me? {spoken in French}

She turns around and looks at me for maybe 30 seconds. Then, her arms are wide open and she calls me by my name; I rush into her solid and warm embrace. We were both so happy to see each other. I mean, how coincidental could this be, finding her in this huge school, two stories full of classrooms, on such a big evening!

PROCEEDING DOWN MEMORY LANE...

We know from daily life that we exist for other people...
First of all for whose smiles and well – being
Our own happiness depends.

~Albert Einstein~

I remember being five, having always bitten my nails and the skin surrounding them, due to much stress in our home. One evening, my dad decided that nothing was ever going to stop me from this bad habit!

He asked me to watch him boil water in a kettle then pour some of it into a cup. Then he asked me to sit at the kitchen table and had me watch him stir the boiled water, slowly, with a spoon. I had no idea what was going to happen!

After a few minutes, he said: "As you do not seem to understand that chewing your nails is not appropriate, I'm going to teach you a lesson you will never forget!"

One or two minutes would go by; he would then have me put my chewed up middle finger, from my right hand, into the hot water.

OH! My goodness, did it ever burn! Each time I'd try to lift my finger up and out of the water, he would scream and talk in a very angry tone and say: "Keep your finger in that cup!"

I would just sit there and cry.

My sister was never punished at a level anywhere near this kind of treatment! She was Daddy's little girl who could do no wrong—all the more to make me angrier over the years!

My mom would be close by, in the living room, watching me suffer. Each time, after my dad had covered my finger with gauze to keep it clean, I would run to hug my mother and ask her to make him stop.

All she ever said was; "Just stop biting your nails!"

★ ★ ★

Although a father like this is very cruel to you as a child, you love him, despite his rage; you also love your mother, because there's nowhere else to turn.

I never really counted on my parents for true comfort.

★ ★ ★

One late afternoon, it started to hail outside; my sister and I followed my mom to every window while she sprayed blessed holy water on all of the curtains of every window while making the sign of the cross, repeating prayers out loud.

I knew my dad was due to be home any minute, and I was frightened, thinking this hail could kill him!

After the storm passed, my dad came into the house. He'd waited in the garage while all these huge chunks of ice cubes fell from the sky. So relieved to see him, I simply ran into his arms, telling him how scared I'd been that he might have died.

Every time he came home from work, he'd kiss my mom twice; being the dramatic child and all, I asked him to kiss me twice also, always looking for his approval. He did so that one time!

Never again did I ask! My dad's behaviour towards me became very disgusting. He'd kiss me on my lips and this ALWAYS felt so wrong and very uncomfortable! He would continue these gestures throughout his lifetime; every single time, I'd feel very uncomfortable in my mind and heart. He would insist over the years that these were kisses from a father to his daughter! Yah! Right!

FRAGMENTED
FEARS

MY PARENTS...

*I just wish people would realize that anything is possible
if you try...dreams are made if people try.*

~Terry Fox~

My parents knew our neighbours, Mr. and Mrs.Quenville and their daughter Madeleine, quite well. First of all, my dad rented a room at the Quenville's home for a few years, along with a few other fellows, who later on became some of his very good friends.

On the other hand, my mom had been Madeleine's friend way before my father entered the picture. Both women were about the same age and went dancing every Saturday night across the river to Detroit city.

Mrs. Quenville was always very nice to both my sister and I, often hanging her clothes outside while her dog, Ginger, kept barking. One day we found out he'd died and saw how sad this made her feel. She was such a lovely person. At times, visiting her as neighbours, she'd often be bedridden, as she'd been ill for many years.

Over the years, my husband and I think we figured out what happened to the trio of Madeleine, my mom, and my dad. Here's our hypothesis: While my dad rented a room in Mrs. Quenville's home, we think he fell in love with Madeleine—but her feelings were not mutual. Then one evening, my mother came by; this is how she met my father. Madeleine introduced them.

It took a good period of time for my dad to build up his courage enough to ask my mom—who was extremely attractive—if she would consider dating him…being quick to mention that he had no talent in the art of dancing!

Soon afterwards, my mom gave up dancing altogether, thinking that maybe now was the time to change her weekly routine; and so began the relationship between my parents.

My mom was looking for financial security, and my dad had a very well-paying job at Chrysler, including many benefits, as he was part of a union back then.

It took my mom two years before she would even consider getting married, because as a child, growing up in the woods of northern Ontario, she had seen my grandfather leave his family to go to the wood camps to cut trees in order to make a living. He would only come home on the weekends.

Once, my grandmother had asked him to stay until she gave birth to the child she was carrying, but to no avail. Days later, my grandmother started having contractions and was screaming with pain; my mom, being the eldest, was asked to run as fast as she could to the local midwife's house, which was maybe a mile or so away. My mom, not knowing anything about childbirth, thought my grandmother was going to die!

Coming back to my parents' story; my mom was very fearful that my dad would leave her in the same predicament, to give birth to their own children without his presence or support!

★ ★ ★

One evening, in 1953, while standing in line to see a movie, my dad took a small box from his inside pocket, opened it up in front of my mom, and asked her to marry him.

My mother looked at the engagement ring; they'd talked about this, so my dad felt confident she would say yes—and she did!

AS FOR MADELEINE...

If you trust life and learn to embrace it
and try not to control everything,
then life can be more wondrous
than you thought it would be.

~Sarah Ban Breathnach~

When my sister and I were ages four and six, we visited her small apartment. For some unknown reason, my mom very strictly told my sister and I to go play outside. We feared going out near the alley that was directly below, and said we'd rather just stay in.

My mom insisted in a very odd way. We both sensed something was wrong although could not figure out what it was. We reluctantly went downstairs and just stood around waiting for my parents to call us back in.

Finally, they appeared outside, took us home, no questions asked. Decades later, I'd figure out most of Madeleine's story.

★ ★ ★

The reason Mr. and Mrs. Quenville were our neighbours, is because upon marrying my mom, my dad bought the house next door to the Quenville's for the sum of $2,000! In those days, not everyone could afford this kind of price for a home. I mean, you've got to remember that when I was born in 1954, it cost one cent to mail a letter!

★ ★ ★

My mom had made her own wedding dress. For my First Communion, she downsized it to fit me, keeping the same pattern. Later on, at the age of ten or so, I was confirmed in the same French-Canadian Catholic Church (St. Jérome)

MY AUNT LILIANNE...

A problem is a chance to do your best.

~Duke Ellington~

My aunt Lilianne had come from work one evening, when I was six, to discuss with my father the sore throat I'd had for over a month. My doctor, after many visits, kept telling my mom I was fine, and that my pain would subside in a short period of time. But this was not the case.

I'd been crying for many weeks, telling my mom that my throat hurt so much. This particular evening, my aunt had my dad call the doctor to order some kind of liquid, which she believed would fight off the infection in my throat.

Oh my god! After my dad paid the pharmacy delivery boy, he read the instructions, which said he had to paint my throat with this purple liquid every few hours. UGH! The taste was absolutely unbearable.

Each time my dad would smear this stuff onto my tongue and into my throat, I would gag then run to the washroom and spit out as much as I could. My dad, being who he was, just kept putting more purple stuff in my throat until I kept it in my mouth. It tasted so bad and felt very dry. I fought him every time, crying my eyes out! He was quite a sadistic person, my impression being that he seemed to take pleasure in seeing me suffer!

Eventually, my mom took me to see another doctor who immediately booked an operating room to remove my tonsils. The day I was admitted, a nurse asked me to undress, put a hospital gown on AND also asked that I remove my panties. I thought she was nuts! In those days that's how it was. I walked down a long hallway into the O.R. with an open gown at the back! I felt so embarrassed!

As we reached the room where the doctor was waiting for me, my mom, all of a sudden, got into an elevator, looking quite upset, as she had not prepared me to be left alone. She felt guilty and I was scared out of my wits! Luckily, the doctor was most reassuring. He then began to administer the anaesthetic (called ether), asked me to count to 100, then backwards to ONE. Soon, all became black.

When I awoke, I'd been placed in a baby's crib AND my throat was 100 times more painful than before the operation! I could barely speak. The one thing I did tell my mom, who'd been in the room when I came to, was that I had to go pee really badly. The nurse in the room said I was not allowed to get out of bed; she then proceeded to give my mom a bedpan. I thought she was also nuts!

It felt like I was being treated like a baby and was very upset, but could not even cry as this made my throat even more unbearable! My mom helped me sit up on this uncomfortable piece of metal and I ended up urinating half in the pan and half on the bed sheets! It seemed like an hour before the nurse brought new linen.

My mom had promised me chocolate ice-cream. Finally discharged from the hospital, I sat on the side of my own bed, waiting for my promised treat. At the same moment, Mrs. Quenville walked quickly past my room, holding a large container of liquid. Now, my mom was not thinking straight as she handed me a glass of this yellowish-coloured liquid, saying it was eggnog. Turns out I did not like eggs and refused to drink the stuff.

I always felt badly over the years, having broken Mrs. Quenville's little heart. My mother had said impatiently: "I should never have told you what was in that glass because it would have given you some strength."

In the end, the chocolate ice-cream was most soothing!

M. L. CARMEN FORCIER

A few years later, Mrs. Quenville passed away and my dad was quite sad, as he'd known her family for many years. My mom decided to take my sister and I to the funeral home; she explained to us that Mrs. Quenville looked like she was sleeping. As we approached the body, she did look at peace—and I noticed something odd about the coffin: it was half-closed, hiding her body from the waist down.

For years to come, I believed that when someone died, their legs were cut off!

ONE EVENING...

All difficulties in your life,
give you opportunities to grow spiritually beyond yourself.
They are a test of your inner strength.

~Victor E. Franklin~

One evening, my aunt Lilianne came over with her boyfriend, a taxi driver who looked very, very scary to me. I screamed when I saw his face, ran to my room, and kept screaming, hidden behind one of my little wooden chairs made by my paternal grandfather. My dad actually let this man into my room to come and scare me even more.

He stooped down, looking at me through the top opening of my chair, and asked me why I was so afraid. I said his eyes were a funny shape that I'd never seen before.

As it turned out, he was Japanese; my aunt had consulted my parents to see if they approved of him if she were to marry him. My dad counselled her by saying she could do much better by choosing someone else.

Eventually, while this same aunt worked in Detroit, she met my future "oncle Jean" (French for "uncle John") with whom I fell in love the first time I met him; I was six years old and could not keep my eyes off him when he arrived at my grandparents' house. He was studying cardiology.

He was so funny, kind, and generous; everyone loved him instantly! He was one of my favourite uncles.

This poem is dedicated to him:

La Première Fois…
Debout là
Devant une fenêtre

Manteau noir
Et foulard blanc
Son être intense
Si ferme, si juste
Mon coeur voyait
Me regardait
Miroir transparent

Assise ici
Avec le temps
Ce souffle de vie
Encore vivant
Manteau noir
Et foulard blanc
Je te vois toujours
Miroir transparent

ENGLISH TRANSLATION

At the window

He stood
So firm and intense..
Long black coat…
With snow white scarf…
So firm so just…
My heart could see
Was looking at me…
Transparent mirror

Sitting here…
In the 'now'
This breath of life

Still lives somehow
Long black coat
With snow white scarf
I see you always…
Transparent mirror

~M.L. Carmen Forcier~
Copyright (1984)

MY
UNFOLDING
UNIVERSE

MASHED POTATOES...

A change of feeling is a change of destiny.

~Nevill Goddard~

Today, I'm now able to eat mashed potatoes—BUT—from the age of two to seven, my mother would serve them dry with no butter and slightly burnt. Throughout these years, almost every night at the dinner table, I remember gagging, always coming so close to vomiting, while my father watched and warned me that I'd better eat them all and not be sick or I'd be sorry!

Finally, after all of those days and years, my mother thought of boiling potatoes; these I could tolerate—finally!

Decades later I shared this thought with my psychiatrist whose response was that even the army does not treat its own soldiers as severely as this!

Another interesting element to my mom's cooking was this: after having served our plates, I witnessed my sister, over a period of years and years, till she was almost fifteen, handing her plate to my dad who then mashed everything up into a pile of mixed food and buried it with enough ketchup to make my sister turn red (smile). Once we were grown and had our own lives, my sister would often repeat how our mom's cooking had always made her feel so sick!

Now that I was in grade one, my mom was insisting I wear my rain boots to school—but I refused. I really disliked wearing those galoshes. They made me look like an old granny, and besides, it was not raining outside! She kept repeating that I would not be able to go to the shoemakers after school with her and my sister if I came home with wet feet.

Of course it just had to rain walking home from school! Upon my arrival, my mother had me take off my shoes and socks then placed my feet near the furnace in the living room. The shoemaker was the last thing on my mind; I'd totally forgotten! All of a sudden, my sister was called to the living room from our bedroom, where she'd been hiding, all dressed to go out with my mom.

Before I could protest, they were out the door and gone!

I immediately ran to my bed and started crying and screaming really loud because I wanted my great-great uncle in the back room to come and comfort me in my misery. After what seemed like a long time I stopped, realising no one was ever coming to rescue me! My mom had succeeded in her punishment!

★ ★ ★

After dinner every night, we would ask if we could please watch Popeye cartoons on TV. Having brushed our teeth, we always sat together in a comfy rocking chair. One early evening, one of my friends, Jenny, came over to watch cartoons. She lived on our street, but we were never allowed to play at her house because it meant crossing a busy road; plus, she lived right near the Detroit River.

She once told me that, in the confessionals in church (where we would go behind a curtain and confess our sins to a priest), there was an actual hole; once you entered past the curtain, the hole would make you fall into hell FOREVER! I explained this to my dad as we were nearing our seats the following Sunday. He took one look at me, SMILED, and never confirmed one way or the other whether this story was true or not; it keep me fearing HELL!

ANY TIME MY SISTER AND I...

All that we send into the lives of others
comes back into our own.

~Edwin Markham~

Anytime my sister and I went shopping with my mom, I'd be crying my eyes out as my feet hurt so very much. They always felt like they were on fire! So the three of us would walk and shop until we found a store with a chair nearby. My mom would explain the situation to the clerks, and I would sit for a while.

She finally took me to see a new doctor and the verdict was that my feet had no arches; they were completely flat! He suggested that my parents exercise my feet on a Coke bottle, rolling them back and forth on the curve of its shape; this never did help!

I'd always worn my nice white booties-type shoes and now my mom bought me a pair of really ugly brown shoes. They were so awful-looking and really long and big, causing my self-image to slowly deteriorate. I would beg my mother to buy me nicer-looking shoes, as these were so embarrassing to wear; they looked like men's shoes. Her answer was always: "No, be quiet, and stop complaining. Make the sacrifice."

Nothing ever really helped my painful feet, so I just learned to live with it, though once in my forties, I discovered orthotics; these I now wear.

Still living in our first house (till I was almost seven), we were often tempted to open the back gate of the yard and play in front of our garage, right in the middle of the alley. My sister liked to find shiny little pieces of broken stones, and my friends and I would go there just for a change of scenery. One day, my dad found us playing there and had an absolute conniption fit!

You see, every so often, this old man we called "the Sheeny Man" would drive through the alleys of our neighbourhoods and collect what looked like junk, heaped up really high in his huge wagon. As always, I was to blame for setting a bad example for my sister; my dad would threaten me by screaming out loud that if I kept playing in the alley, "the Sheeny Man" would pick me up, put me in his wagon, kidnap me, and I'd disappear forever! His threat worked for me, although my sister would continue to go out there anyway; she had no fear whatsoever of my father!

REMEMBERING...

As we look toward the dawn,
our spirit rises high, on wings of certainty.
We will share eternity.
This is how it's meant to be-
For life goes on, and we must be strong.

~Bob Quinn~

One year at Christmas, while in kindergarten/grade one, my dad had gone all out and bought my sister and I a record player with several small red "45s." We were absolutely thrilled. On another occasion, he'd bought us a mini snooker table and showed us how to play this game by the rules. It was fun.

Only my dad took the time to play with us once in a while. My mom was always way too busy, so we learned never to disturb her. I remember begging my dad to play war with a deck of cards or even to play snakes and ladders; he always consented. Eventually we learned how to play crib and would sometimes even beat him! He taught me how to read time and how to tie an apron from the back.

In later years, he built a ping pong table; here again, I would at times beat him!

My cousin Richard (second love) would come to see us at this happy time of year, with his sister Line, my aunt and uncle. For many years, Richard and I danced the twist to the tune of "Jingle Bell Rock" which his dad always sang for us. It was our "love dance" you might say. After searching my heart over the years, I finally remembered these few good memories!

(As a small child, my true love was Pat Boone, the actor, whom I'd seen on television, standing in an old cabin)

MY GREATEST PLEASURE...

To trigger love, think kind thoughts,
show affection towards your family and friends,
listen to inspirational music.

~M.L. Carmen Forcier~

My greatest pleasure was to colour with crayons. OH! The joy of using red was always such a great pleasure! My older cousin Pauline would often colour with me while she baby-sat; this made me very happy! She taught me how to outline the dark lines already on the pages; this helped me avoid going over the already-printed lines.

One Christmas, my parents had given me a blackboard with white chalk. What a thrill that was. I loved writing from the time I was four. This may have been the beginning of my love for words. Writing neatly would come later!

I remember one birthday party my mom had for me as a small child; most of my cousins were invited to celebrate either my birthday or my sister's. My mom would take pictures and watch as we opened our many gifts. Then, she would serve cake and ice-cream. There are a few pictures in one of my photo albums reminding me of one such party. This is one of the few memories where I remember my mom being somewhat nice, although rather impatient, having to deal with all of my little guests!

One day, my mom left my sister and I to play at my aunt Peggy's with her six children, plus another aunt's four kids. After being there for a few hours, my cousin Paul pushed and hit his brother Melvin. I intervened and slapped Paul, trying to defend Melvin.

My aunt ran out of the house, slapping me on the wrist saying, "You do not get involved with other people's battles. Let them fight their own!"

Although I could not understand what she meant at the time, I got the gist of her message later on.

★ ★ ★

As my sister and I were playing with our toys in our backyard, the next-door neighbour, Mr. Smith, came to the fence between our yards and started yelling at both of us for mistreating our mom.

"What?" we said to ourselves.

Finally, I understood that my mom had complained to him, describing us as very disobedient brats—and had asked if he could talk some sense into us! Can you believe this?

She continued to do so with other people, over the next few years.

IN 1961...

How we spend our days is of course how we spend our lives.

~Annie Dillard~

In 1961, we moved from our first old house into a brand new one, designed to my parents' specifications and constructed by a hired builder. Finally, after eight long years, they'd saved enough money for their dream home. My parents bought new furniture for the living, dining and kitchen areas.

Having new surroundings also meant new friends.

This big move, we knew, also meant a new school, and that we would be traveling there on a school bus. On the first day, the bus was about twenty minutes late (with standing room only); my mom, who had stood there waiting with us, gave the bus driver real live heck for being so late. He explained that he'd gotten stuck in some mud!

There it was—my mom's anger towards the bus driver, on the first day of school, in front of all those new kids. What a horrible embarrassment this was for both my sister and I! She always acted in ways that made us feel ashamed that she was our mother.

THERE WERE TIMES...

It is in the HEART of matters
through which we feel the BREATH of life.

~M.L. Carmen Forcier~

There were times when my father would be so enraged that even my mom feared him. One summer afternoon in 1961 (I was almost seven and my sister five), my mom sat us down on the sofa of the den; she sat between us while my father walked around the house, ranting, raving and screaming back and forth. My mom had her arms around both my sister and I, crying softly, telling us not to say one word, for this would have set my dad off to express even more anger. We never did understand that outbreak.

That same summer, I had a great idea: I wanted to write a book, a love story. So I took a small piece of paper and wrote,

'Walking along the beach hand in hand with John'...

Then I ran out of inspiration (smile) and placed the thought in my bedside drawer; I forgot it was there after a while.

But have no fear—Mom is here!

Maybe four to five months went by; one night at the supper table, my mom started telling my dad about how I'd written dirty thoughts which she'd found in my bedside drawer.

I said to myself: *what is she talking about?*

She was livid and my dad was furious! He immediately said I'd have to confess this "MORTAL sin."

Finally, remembering the slight beginnings of my first attempt at writing, I was really scared! It was in vain for me to try explaining what my intentions had been as this was all just "sex garbage" to both of them (as a team)! I was not even asked one single question!

The next day, I confessed my sin to the priest, knelt in front of Jesus, reciting my penance, forever carrying my fear of hell.

NOW...THE FASHION INDUSTRY...

*People who say it cannot be done
should not interrupt those who are doing it.*

~Unknown~

The fashion industry was introducing the mini-skirt. Well, you should have seen my sister and I cut our uniform skirts (black and white checkers) so that when we wore them they *just* barely covered our behinds; and *then* we would have the nerve to cross our legs in the classroom!

I tell you, my mother nearly went crazy during those "last of the hippie years" as she was such a fanatically religious person; these skirts represented to her one of the most evil things that had ever hit society; she blamed us almost every day, repeating that we were under the influence of the devil.

Of course, there was no way we could go to school if we did not wear a mini skirt! Everyone was wearing them, and we would have been the laughingstock of the whole student body! Even the teachers wore them!

★ ★ ★.

One day, my mom even walked into the back door with a big crucifix on a stick in her hand, extended away from her face, with Jesus facing my way; she was screaming her brains out by saying that my sister and I were

BEING BIPOLAR

driving her crazy! She was SO ANGRY…she truly looked like someone who'd lost her mind!

AT THE AGE OF SEVEN....

*Learn to feel you've earned your way here
wherever that may be.*

~ M.L. Carmen Forcier~

You've accomplished so much in your life!

~Carmen~

In October of 1961, for the first time in my life, I discovered my immense love for books, and reading became m.y passion!

One weekend, in the beginning of the school year, I'd brought two library books home, and my father noticed I was not reading them. He asked me about this and my answer was: "Well, I'm unable to read them, as I left the book I started reading in my desk at school; I cannot read two books at one time!"

He laughed and said that when I became older I would be able to read many books, all at once. As for him, I was curious as to why he never read a book, and his response was that he'd read for so very many years and then got to a point where he got so obsessed, he wanted to read almost everything he could find. So, he decided to stop reading altogether and would often tell me over the years, that one day, I would understand. My father, being the sadist that he was, punished himself by totally banning books from his life.

* * *

While living in this dream home of my parents, I would constantly ask my mom and dad if we could have a small pool, maybe a little bit bigger than the one we had as small children. The heat in Windsor is so often unbearable as it is extremely humid.

One day, my mother got fed up with my ongoing asking. She pointed to a small metal silver tub (in which there was standing room only, for one person) that she filled with water. Then, still holding the hose, she started showering me up and down and sideways; the water was freezing cold!

She then said: "There! Are you satisfied?"

I was mortified!

My sister and friends watched the whole darn show and laughed at me the whole time!

* * *

On certain evenings, our neighbours would be cooking hot dogs outside in their back yard while my sister and I kept looking towards them while eating our own dinner. After we'd almost finished eating the food on our plates, my dad would say: "OK—go on. Go get some hot dogs."

This was our thrill of a lifetime as my dad never did do BBQs.

MYSTIFYING
MOMENTS

NEARING MY EIGHTH
BIRTHDAY...

*The fragrance always remains
in the hand that gives the rose*

~Hada Bejar~

We are spiritual beings surrounded by our beautiful human bodies.

~common thought~

In1962, my mother noticed dark brown leathery patches of skin, all on the left side of my body. I was too young to notice anything different about myself. In the meantime, she'd written to my most cherished uncle, who was studying to be a cardiologist, (in California U.S.A.) explaining what she saw developing. When she received his letter of response, he seemed to know that I had some kind of skin problem, most likely called scleroderma, a connective tissue disease. He suggested my mom take me to Henry Ford Hospital as soon as possible!! This hospital was across the Detroit River, in the outskirts of Detroit City, U.S.A. My mom, having made an appointment with this hospital, took me across on a Greyhound bus. I was so afraid she was going to leave me at the hospital. I prayed my little heart out, to be taken back home with her, after the doctors examination. Finally, a nurse called out my name; as my mother took my hand to follow the nurse, the latter said that she would take me to see the specialist herself, and that my mother could wait in the lobby! THAT was kind of odd, as this was a huge hospital!!...I could have easily been kidnapped or even worse!

The doctor I saw was Chinese looking and examined my leathery brown spots, commenting here and there, words I did not understand. He asked me if these areas were hurting me in any way and I said no. (I still not having noticed anything different about my left arm)

The nurse then brought me back to my mom in the lobby of the hospital, where we waited for what seemed forever, expecting the doctor to come and explain to her his observations of my skin. No one ever came! Finally, my mom got up enough courage to go to the front desk receptionist, to inquire about this doctor of mine. The receptionist was a young fellow; he started making phone calls trying to locate someone who could assist him in finding this MD, to explain to my mom what my diagnosis was. Then, all of a sudden, my mom started crying, explaining that my dad had been on strike for 3 months! My whole heart sank so deeply, to the bottom of my stomach, as it hurt me so much to see my mom in tears, actually saying my parents did not have any insurance to have me admitted to a U.S. hospital as a patient.

After a good 15 to 20 minutes, my mom seemed to have received an answer and we left the lobby; she walked to a pay phone, specifically telling me to stay out of hearing range while she called my dad, to explain what the message from the doctor had been! Now, I was not aware of any danger as I still had not noticed my brown areas, and after waiting a long time, finally, my dad came to pick us up and I ran into his arms, knowing for sure that I was not going to be admitted to the hospital as a patient! He said: "Hey! What are you doing here?"(As if I did not suspect my mom had called him)...I was so happy to go back home that the rest of the trip is a total blank in my mind!

My mother re-wrote a letter to my uncle, re-explaining my situation, and my uncle's second response was that he highly recommended that my mom take me to Sick Kids Hospital, in Toronto, Ontario, Canada. A few months later, my mother and I were on a train, going to Toronto Ontario, a 4 hour drive by car from Windsor, my hometown.

PS

Being the only child on the train, the ticket man showed me the whole of it, from one end to another. Some cars had skylights; this he mentioned, was a more expensive car. In my own child's mind, I thought, woe, there's no one sitting here, it's totally empty…why could we not just sit there instead of in the more simple seats my mom and I were in?

Afterwards, at the first stop, I was helped out of the train by the same man, who then took my hand and brought me to the engineers who were driving the train. I climbed into their very small quarters and of course, I was treated with a lot of affection. I was immensely honoured and excited, being this special centre of attention!

WE ARRIVED IN TORONTO…

The pessimist complains about the wind, the optimist expects it to change,
And the realist adjusts the sail.

~William Arthur Ward~

Around 7pm., in mid-October, it was dark and my mother had planned that we stay at a YMCA, in order that we have a place to sleep and eat. Upon arriving, a gentleman told us there were no vacant rooms.

(My mother had not reserved ahead of time. She acted on pure faith, which sometimes can hit you in the face!)

Anyways, the same gentleman told us to wait a few moments while he went out to see what he could find! When he came back he said to my mom:

I've found you a place in an old Jewish woman's home. She's agreed to take you in for as many days as you need.

What a relief!! He accompanied us to this woman's home, a short walk from the YMCA, holding an umbrella, as it was pouring rain.

When we came upon the house that would be our haven for about 3 days, the older woman opened the door and welcomed us. We thanked the gentleman (for this miracle) and then entered the house. This woman showed my mother and I a beautiful bedroom where she said I could sleep. I just could not leave my mother's side, as I was so very frightened; so it was agreed that my mom and I would sleep in the older woman's own double bed, together! She was most kind, as she had back problems, and her heart went out to me, for she agreed to sleep in the room she'd shown us, willing to give up her comfort for little me.

The next morning, my mom and I took a streetcar to the Hospital for Sick Kids because we had an appointment to see a few specialists. As we walked down a hallway of this hospital, I smelled my first whiff of sickness and saw some kids in leg casts etc...I was absolutely terrified at the thought that my mother had tried to prepare me to accept to stay in this hospital, if it were required by the doctors, in case they had a treatment for my left arm including the other brown areas on the left side of my body.

Upon arriving in one of the large rooms of the hospital, there were at least 6-8 doctors, waiting to examine me. They all wore white coats, which made the situation look really serious (even though white coats were still a comfort to me).

One of the doctors was a woman and upon examination, hesitated to touch my left arm. I wanted to scream, I'm not a leper!!!! But I said nothing. It would be my first time, to really notice my left arm, with its dark brown leathery patches, going from my hand up to my upper left shoulder! I was more than shocked and did not understand what the doctors were telling my mother. I was so afraid she would go away and just leave me there. As it turned out, on our way back to the Jewish woman's home, my mother explained to me, that the doctors had not seen a case like mine in 35 years and were quite perplexed! They had diagnosed me as having a disease called 'scleroderma' which occurs to one in a million people, for which there really is no treatment available! They asked my mother to call them in 3 days, as this would give them time to consult other doctors.

Three days passed; my mom was about to phone one of the doctors I'd seen AND she did not want me to be in the same room with her while she made the call. She looked at me with such fear in her eyes.

I was absolutely stunned!! Convinced I had a terrible RARE incurable disease, my thoughts were of being left alone in this huge hospital. I remember being taken from the living room to the kitchen by 2 of the older woman's sisters. They sat me on the kitchen counter and asked me if I wanted an orange crush?

After pouring me a glass of this fizzy drink, they handed it to me. To my utter surprise, it was very delicious! Finally, after about what seemed like 20 to 30 minutes, the sisters led me back to the living room to see my mom who now had a devastated expression on her face. All she said to me was that we were going home together, that I was not going back to that hospital! My God, I never felt so relieved and happy in my whole life!!

During the phone call, doctors had said to my mom, they could try pigs' skin grafts to attempt to cover my dark brown patches. This was all they could offer as a temporary solution, adding that there were no guarantees!! My mom had refused the doctors' suggestion as she explained to me that my arm did not hurt…did not handicap me in any way. So, she decided to take me home and pray!

BEING THE RELIGIOUS FANATIC...

Oh child! Never allow your heart to harden.
Welcome the unicorn into your garden.

~Phyllis Gottlieb~

My mom, during the trip back home, took from her purse some St. Joseph blessed holy healing oil that she'd once purchased from a certain priest. She rubbed the oil on my skin and asked me to pray to St Anne to help me heal from this misunderstood and rare disease!

The doctors she'd spoken to mentioned she might try using cocoa butter in order to keep my arm lubricated. They'd also said that there would be atrophy of this arm and possibly some to the whole left side of my body!

Back in Windsor, my mom explained the details of our visit to my dad, who from that day forward, massaged my left arm with the cocoa butter every evening in the hopes of strengthening my arm, attempting to avoid atrophy. As it turned out, after that one year, he stopped because there had been no change in my arm s size.

This disease became a nightmare for me. The kids at school started noticing my dark brown leathery arm and always laughed at me, calling me names I'm ashamed to repeat; they were so cruel!!! That's when I decided I would no longer wear short sleeves, AT ALL TIMES ('til the age of 25), including summers, which are extremely hot in Windsor and very humid from being surrounded by the 3 great lakes, located near Lake Erie and sitting on the Detroit River!

There I was in 2nd and 3rd grades and from that day forward, whenever it was recess at school, I dreaded going outside as every kid around, ridiculed me and chose not to play anywhere near my body, in case they got my cooties!!!

Everywhere my family visited, my mom would show my left arm to everyone and explain my story over and over again. Meanwhile, every time someone examined my left arm (afraid to touch me) it made my complex that much worse. I do not blame my mom for doing this; she personally needed support on this sad subject. This went on for some time until everyone known to my parents, knew of my rare skin disease! I always felt so self-conscious of my body, never wore a 2 piece bathing suit and as a teenager, went roller skating in a very hot arena, every summer evening, wearing long sleeved winter woollen sweaters.

WHAT MY FATHER TOLD ME...

Being oneself...is really the essence of all wisdom.

~Roland Goodchild~

.... at the age of 22, was that my uncle, the cardiologist to whom my mother had written, re: the scleroderma had told my parents, as well as my grand-parents, (totally unbeknownst to me) that due to this rare illness, I would not live to see my 17th birthday!

On my 55th birthday, in October in 2009, I realised some kind of miracle happened while I was growing up; the dark patches of skin had lightened over time. My arm never hurt and I did not turn into stone {as it is predicted this disease is capable of doing.} Although my left arm has remained atrophied, and the left side of my body is slightly smaller than my right side, I am most grateful that I've always had a left arm at all—plus, my mom would remind me that I never had a spot of this brownish leathery skin on my face! Thank you dear Universe!!!

Also, had I known as a child, I might have worn some type of jewellery in order to honour my left hand; as it turned out, today, my left arm is about half the size of my right arm, skinny, with no fat, compared to my right arm which is chubbier and looks normal. I used to refer to my left hand as my 80 year old looking hand having developed many big veins right away. (It was smaller and skinnier than my other hand.) My right hand, I named my good hand for it had retained its young appearance.

{Nowadays, I tend to wear lots of jewellery and it so happens that some rings I have, only come in smaller sizes. So now, I've found an advantage to the smaller fingers of my left hand!!}

One of the things to watch for if you have scleroderma is; 'Am I having trouble swallowing?' This question was asked of me by every doctor I'd ever had. My answer was always no, until one day, in 1982, at the age of 28, I was in a hospital cafeteria, unable to initiate the process of swallowing! Soon after, I saw my Internist, Dr. Henry Ballon, a nephrologist, the one doctor who had made me promise never to look up the disease I had (for the rest of my life), as it would only scare me!! I explained my problem to him, and his exact response was…"Do you know how very serious this is??" I then told him what my GP had said about scleroderma patients.

When they get to a certain age, they can no longer swallow any type of food or drink and choke on themselves, thereby needing to be in hospital, hooked to an intravenous tube for feeding, waiting for death! When Dr. Ballon heard this, he was livid with anger, as he'd never discussed the seriousness of my illness with me, for fear my thoughts could trigger my body into getting worse! He then said that he would have a very serious talk with my GP. From then on my GP never spoke of my illness again.

Although in previous years, he had mentioned that I'd be the only patient he'd ever see, with scleroderma! The trouble with my swallowing process would come later.

PS

One really profound lesson I learned from having this disease is that I have never made fun of anyone I've met or spoken to, who had either a physical or mental handicap and not for any other reason, for that matter. Something to remember!

SOON AFTER ARRIVING....

From the beginning of life to its end,
Love is the only emotion which matters.

~June Callwood~

.... from Toronto, my mom accompanied me to piano lessons, every Saturday morning, for about 6 months. The teacher only lived one block away from us. She held classes in her private home and for the first few years, it cost my mom $1.00 for my half hour lessons. I remember holding a $1 dollar bill, folded twice on itself, in my left hand, carrying my music books in my right. My mom's biggest dream had always been to play the piano; by observing my lessons, she would memorize what my music teacher taught me and started to play easy songs at home, from my first kindergarten book.

My parents had bought a used electric piano, which was so cool, as it had a particular tinny sound. This electrical instrument had been at my grand-parents' house for a few years. As soon as we moved into my parents dream home this instrument was moved into our new dining room.

From my lessons, I learned some theory and scales and also participated in exams for grades 4, 6 and 8. These were held in a quiet room some-where downtown and were pretty nerve wracking. Although I passed with good marks for grades 4 and 6, I barely passed the grade 8 exams!! My teacher phoned my mom and asked if there was anything wrong? Had I practiced enough? Turns out, I remember my concentration, during this time, was not the greatest and I'd always hated practicing in the first place! There I was, eventually playing classical music, such as Beethoven, Chopin, Mozart, when all I really wanted to learn was how to play the Beatles, the Rolling Stones…

IN 1963...

*We all have been given a gift of one kind or another;
it is important to realize and utilize those gifts
for the benefit of mankind.*

~Kelly Meyer~ (activist)

At the tender age of 9, on one of the many occasions where I'd find myself being yelled at by my dad, I did something to myself; something most serious!! After one of his screaming spells, he went out on an errand; when he came backhe absolutely went absolutely crazy, looking at my eyes, screaminghis head off. His voice was so loud! He put his large hand on my forehead, tilted my head back repeating; "You took them all out. What have you done to your eyes?? Why have you done this horrible thing??" I was totally terrified, as I did not know why I'd pulled out every single eyelash from both eyes top and bottom. My dad asked me to go and look at myself in the mirror!! I looked very odd with swollen and puffy eyes, with a hint of a Chinese look. This depressed me Very Much!!! My mom looked it up in the dictionary and told me that it was going to take 3 months before my eyelashes would all grow back in! This was devastating information for me!!

A few days later, my mother said something to the effect that my aunt Lilianne was coming to visit soon and would I ever look horrible in front of her!! Interestingly enough, when my favourite aunt visited, I'm sure she noticed my eyes, as it was SO obvious, although she was kind enough to not say one word. What a huge relief!!!

This habit of punishing myself went off and on for years;

I truly felt a lot of satisfaction in seeing the roots of each eyelash as if I'd accomplished something important!

One Sunday afternoon we were visiting with friends of the family. The wife, Mrs Laliberté, took one look at me and began badgering my mom with the same question, over and over again;

"What's wrong with Carmen's eyes?"

I kept pleading and pleading my mom with my big brown eyes, to PLEASE not answer her question!! Finally, she broke down and told her what I'd done. I was so mortified!!!! How could she tell this mean woman, my deepest secret!!! I cried and cried and cried. That's when my dad and his friend George came in from the back-yard. George asked why was I crying? After pausing, my father told him, adding that it was a mystery to both my parents as to why I was doing this to myself!!!

Mrs. Laliberté took advantage of the situation and gave me heck for at least 5 minutes' time, as angry as can be, continuously asking me why I kept doing this to myself? I did not speak a word all the way home.

Shortly afterwards, Maybelline came out with a new mascara and every time I saw this commercial on television, where the girl went from having plain lashes to the full length beautiful mascara lash look, I promised myself that one day I would also have very long lashes with the help of this particular mascara!

This stressful situation depressed me to no end!! When I began high school, close to the age of 12, I thought of a way to camouflage my no lash look, by using a navy coloured pencil to draw a thin line above my eyelashes (unaware of any kind of make-up at the time).

They would slowly grow back in, and yet, I continued with this very addictive habit; learned to wear false eyelashes with absolutely nothing to hold them in place!! Now there's a mystery if ever there was one!! Eventually, my eyelashes grew back in, fully, AND they were even longer than before!

M. L. CARMEN FORCIER

One evening, I snuck into the washroom to use my mom's mascara, which consisted of a small brush, which you used to dip into a black dry cake with a little water.

My sister and I went to church that evening (it was Lent).

I chose to sit at the back of the church and NOT go to communion for fear my mom's acquaintances would see my huge brown mascara eyes; it was that noticeable!!!! This made me very happy and relieved!!! Finally, I had my dream! I looked like the Maybelline girl in the TV commercial!!

MOST OF MY MOM'S FAMILY...

You tend to hit where you aim, so aim high!

~Bob Templeton~

...lived in Windsor. During my dad's summer holidays, we would always go to Sudbury, Ontario, where my dad's family lived. It was 467 miles away; my sister and I constantly repeated; "Are we there yet?"

In the summer of 1963, at the age of 9, my dad took us to visit one of his first cousins, who lived close to his own family. She was the mom of 6 kids and one of them was called Jocelyn--I loved her as well as her name, right from the first glance. After we all begged our parents for my sister and I to stay overnight, it was finally agreed that ok, yes wed won. What a thrill and a half! Jocy and I, as well as both our sisters, talked the night away until 4am or so! As we were in the basement, we did not think we could be heard from upstairs! Then out of the blue, Jocy's mom appeared at the top of the stairs, sternly saying to all of us, that we had to sleep now as it was very late!!! I think we kept the conversation going for another hour or so and finally drifted off to sleep around 4am. What a great night that was because this is where Jocy and I bonded and became best friends. It was almost time for everyone else in Jocy's family to get up; I believe we slowly woke up around noon!!

My parents came by to pick us up around 7pm the next day. Jocy and I, being second cousins, actually strengthened our friendship.

THAT SAME SUMMER...

Life holds us like the moon and the sea. Far, far apart;
the image of the moon shines in the sea, yours in my heart.

~Laura Thompson~

....my dad bought my sister and I our first 2 wheel bikes (2nd hand)...He painted mine turquoise, which is probably why it's still my favourite colour. I was more than thrilled. My father had put big wooden blocks on my pedals because he'd bought the biggest bike, one in which I would grow into. It took me a few weeks but I finally learned how to ride it! This made me very happy!! FREEDOM AT LAST!

Even so, the tension in our home had always been so very depressing. It was truly unbearable!! My parents fought with each other, my sister and I in constant battle with both of them, disagreeing on everything; they in turn would yell at us, my sister and I fought with each other. We had never behaved well enough, nor had we ever done well enough in school.

And again, in 4th grade, I ran up to my father arriving home from school one day to let him know that I'd gotten 100% on my final French Composition Examination!!

Do you know what he said to me?? His response was:

"Oh!! You can do WAY better than that!!!"

Gizèle and I could never do anything that pleased our parents; NOTHING!! EVER!! There was a constant atmosphere of anger and rejection in our family in which, figuratively speaking, we could hardly breathe, the tension was so high!!!

My dad especially, called me names....ENDLESSLY!!!

"You little demon, you little f**** bitch...

Your head is so damned square....Your head is full of rocks....You little f**** disobeying sinner..."

"You god-damned little piece of shit...

You f**** asshole....Eat shit you stupid b****....

You're such a slob....bastard...little f****demon" on and on.

--

My mom criticized everything and everyone under the sun. I have never heard a kind word from her in regards to her acquaintances including both sides of our family members. She's never spoken a positive word about anyone--EVER!! She would yell her head off, every day, as soon as we'd arrive from school, putting my dad down, SCREAMING the same words;

"Your dad is just a lowly Chrysler employee, an ordinary worker who will never make more money in the future years to come!!!"

PS

Just in passing, the night the Beatles sang for the first time on the Ed Sullivan Show, my dad woke my sister and I, to let us witness these four guys with (long hair) groovy music and good looks.

It was February of 1964. I was 9 years old. My father said we'd be seeing them again, for a long time to come! My first choice had always been Paul McCartney! Today, Ringo is my Star!

IN 4TH GRADE…

Let us be grateful to people who make us happy;
they are the charming gardeners who make our souls blossom.

~Marcel Proust~

……I started collecting quotes and have done so ever since. This habit actually originated when I was in grade 4; my teacher, Monsieur Brissette, whom I also had in grade 6, taught me the beauty of words and the wonderful sounds they make when spoken aloud, especially in the French language.

Nowadays, I read and collect quotes all the time. They've encouraged me to be grateful for everyone, everything, especially for my own being of life!

Also, during the beginning of these years, we, the students, were writing on a map of Canada, the names of all of the provinces. My hand- writing was big and messy as I would erase and start over. Monsieur Brissette walked up to my desk so disgusted with what he saw that he told me I'd have to start my work over as it was so sloppy and dirty! From that moment on, I swore to myself that I would have such beautiful hand-writing that one day, people would give me compliments on this, time and time again. I've constantly been aware of the way I form my letters; to this day people in banks, shopping malls, friends and acquaintances etc., will often comment and say: "My goodness, do you ever have beautiful hand-writing!!

By the time I got to grade 7, at the age of 12, my writing skills had continued to improve with every essay, book report or composition. I found this out by pure chance!!

Approximately one week before the end of that school year, our French teacher, Mlle Trottier announced that she would be giving us our last assignment the next day.

And so, the next morning with heightened curiosity, we waited to hear the teacher explain her surprise assignment to the class. As it turned out, she pulled up a shade that had covered the blackboard and we all notice 3 numbered subjects. The teacher then turned around and said; "You have 90 minutes to write a story on one of these 3 topics" Scrap paper as well as sheets of nicer paper were handed out to all students. Now, we were on the clock. / I remember choosing one of the 3 subjects, beginning my story on my scrap paper, so as to compose my story, knowing I would have to re-write the whole thing on the nicer presentable paper. Finally, always checking the clock, I noticed there was only ½ hour left of the 90 minute limit. So there I was, hurrying to finish my work and quickly copying it onto the smooth white sheet of paper. I was writing so fast, on and on. It was nerve wracking to say the least. Finally, I finished one minute before the bell rang.

Time was up! Whew! I said to myself; close call!!

The following week this teacher handed out our compositions back to us by placing them on our desk, right in front of our eyes. She kind of slapped mine down in an angry manner. PLOOF! There was my mark, written on the first blank page. My eyes saw 70% and my whole body and mind sank into a temporary depression!! I'd never had such a low mark, in any subject, EVER, let alone in composition!! I had been saying to myself that my mark would get in the upper 95% or more because I knew I'd written such a great story; one of the best I'd ever written!

On the last day of school, I took my courage in both my hands

(as we say in French) and walked to my teacher's desk.

My question in regards to the low mark of my essay was very important to ask because my family and I were moving out of this particular school district and I would never see this teacher again! Once everyone was gone, I was the only pupil left standing. So afraid was I to ask why I'd gotten such a low mark yet compellingly, I knew I HAD TO ASK MY QUESTION!!

There it was, out in the open: "Why did you give me such a low mark?" I was so nervous; my mouth felt dry, I could hardly bare to hear her answer! This was her response...

"I do not know how you found out the 3 topics on the blackboard but YOU my dear, have cheated. YOU wrote your story at home, before coming in today and simply re-wrote it on the nicer paper, for the full 90 minutes!!"

I could not believe what I'd just heard. I'd ALWAYS been one of the best students in all my years in school and known to be very honest and trust-worthy! I started to explain to her that I could NEVER have known what her 3 subjects were going to be on the board!! It was simply impossible!! She cut me short and re-phrased her answer in an angrier tone;

"DO NOT TELL ME YOUNG LADY WHAT I KNOW FOR SURE. YOU CHEATED BECAUSE NO ONE BUT NO ONE,

CAN WRITE A STORY THIS GREAT IN 90 MINUTES"

This is where I pulled myself up and walked away from her desk. I just could not believe this woman? I stopped saying anything by now as I had just found out that I was this really good writer! It did not matter whether she believed me or not!! I knew the truth and the truth was that I had not cheated and had written a magnificent story in one hour!!! My goodness, I was no longer depressed!! I walked out of this classroom with my story in hand, one of the proudest moments in my life!

{This copy of my greatest story is nowhere to be found)

PS

Speaking only for myself, BIPOLAR illness can tend to make one empha-
size GREATLY what she/he wants to express!!

THE DRAMA OF IT ALL!!!

NATURAL
NEEDS

BETWEEN THE AGES OF EIGHT TO SIXTEEN…

My ability to have abundance in my life -
lies in my ability to forgive.

~Bob Proctor~

Between the ages of eight to sixteen, I would wake up during the middle of most nights, and run to the washroom while calling for my dad. I'd have my head bent towards the inside of the toilet, feeling extremely nauseated, yet always waiting for my dad to take my hand and give me permission to throw-up!

I really could not be sick before he told me it was OK. I'd spit up fountains of undigested food!

Due to the humungous relief and exhaustion I felt afterwards, I'd climb back into bed, very weak, and then I slept very deeply.

Later on, I was to read in medical books that this vomiting may have been related to my having scleroderma.

Having read a book on this illness, it was written that those who have this disease are usually unable to conceive; if they do, then a miscarriage is more than likely to occur!

ONE DAY, AGED NINE, IN GRADE FOUR...

Nothing destroys spirit like poverty.

~ from the film ~ Becoming Jane~

One day, when I was aged nine and in grade four, a young boy arrived as a new student, having moved from North Bay Ontario. The year was 1963. When I went home and told my dad, he looked like he'd seen a ghost! He asked me if I knew the name of this kid's father.

The next day, I approached Donald in the schoolyard and asked him what his father's name was' he said, "Lorenzo."

Upon arriving home that day, I went to my dad's little workshop in our basement, repeating this name to him. Well, my dad just could not believe his ears!

He said, "Are you sure?"

I said "YES, I'm positive!"

He then took his right hand and repeated a funny gesture he always made when he was surprised or learned something new. The palm of his hand went straight to his forehead and he then rocked his head back, showing how stunned and numbed he was!

"Do you know that I grew up with Lorenzo Lanthier in Sturgeon Falls, Ontario, where I was born?" he told me. This was like a miracle!

The following Sunday, there stood two best friends who'd been separated for over forty-five years!

Our parents started visiting each other to play cards. When they came to our place, Donald would sometimes come with them and sit and watch TV with myself and my sister; of course, this was TRUE LOVE (smile). The times he chose not to come, he would call me on the phone, and we'd talk for an hour or more.

His favourite song back then, was "G- L - O - R- I - A!" He just went nuts hearing it! He would always be tapping his hands on his knees to its rhythm, as if he were on drums.

One day soon thereafter, I'd said to our teacher, M. Brissette that Donald and I were going to be getting married one day!

He just broke out in this really wide smile and said, "You'll see; you'll change your mind with time."

I said, "No way!" and this just made him laugh even harder! Cute, hey?

Actually, Donald was my third love, as I'd always been in love with my first cousin, Richard. Ever since we could remember, we'd always felt close. Our families saw this attraction and affection and therefore we were very often reminded that we could not marry each other as cousins, because it meant that our children would be deformed. At one point in time, at the ages of fourteen or fifteen, we both said to each other, "You know, if you were not my cousin, I would marry you!"

★ ★ ★

As an adult, I saw an Oprah Show, where the subject was 'marrying first cousins' Apparently, the show was saying that first cousins could marry and have normal children that would not necessarily develop deformities as believed for so many generations in the past. A doctor in the audience confirmed this myth of deformed babies occurring in first cousins who married to be untrue!

★ ★ ★

The following year, my first baby-sitting job was for Mr. and Mrs. Thibert. I was only ten years old! She would give me fifty cents an hour while she went to church half a block away. I grew to know her three children quite well as I baby-sat them until I was almost seventeen.

AROUND 1966...

*I am the stillness of the now
and I feel the motion of the moment to moment.*

~M. L. Carmen Forcier~

Around 1966, my sister was ten and I was twelve. My aunt Lilianne and uncle John, the cardiologist) lived in Chicoutimi, Québec. On one particular occasion, they'd asked my parents (in advance) to baby-sit their two small children for three weeks, as they wanted to take a holiday in California.

So, my parents agreed, and must have gotten a pretty penny for doing so. I remember my mom being very impatient with both little ones. Pierre was about three and Lucie was a baby, still eating in a high chair and playing in a crib. My mom was always totally exhausted by the end of each day, and of course my dad would scream at Lucie whenever she cried to make her shut up; with his loud thundering voice, all it did was scare her even more.

My mom continued her hairdressing and also continued to sew. The only time she gave these little ones any attention was when she dressed and fed them. That's it! She was indifferent to them and it was never healthy for my sister and I to see my parents acting like this in front of other children. We knew our own fate, if we disobeyed.

Seeing this kind of attitude repeated on others caused us to move further and further away from any kind of relationship with our mom and dad; we did not trust them, and never did confide in them, either. Ever since we could remember, they'd made a habit of punishing us for every little detail of our behaviour.

When my aunt and uncle came back from their trip, they took my parents out for dinner and Gizèle and I took care of our two little cousins; I was eleven, Gizèle was nine! The next morning, my aunt wanted to pay us, and I immediately said, "OH! NO! That's OK!"

★ ★ ★

Being in grade five, I'd found a friend at school; her name was Michelle. She asked me few weeks later if I would like to accompany her to ballet lessons downtown every Saturday afternoon. My parents said it was OK, and so she and I became good friends for a little over two years. This was while we were both in grades five and six, sharing the same classes as well as the same teachers. Sometimes the teacher would prefer her instead of me, or vice-versa, and this started creating a bit of friction between us, as we were competing to be teacher's pet.

I wanted Michelle to see my good-looking uncle Jean. And so one day, on our lunch hour, we ran from the school to my house in order to share this meal with everyone there. Pierre fell in love with Michelle and said he was going to marry her when he grew up. My uncle drove us back to school and I got to sit right beside him in the car! This was very special for me!

When he stopped to let us out, he said, "If you and Gizèle ever need to buy lunch at school, here's eight dollars," which meant four dollars each for both my sister and myself. Only later did I figure out that this money had been given to us for having watched over their children the night they took my parents out for dinner. We considered this a small fortune!

BEING IN THE HABIT…

Weeping may remain for a night,
but rejoicing comes in the morning

~Psalm 30:5~

I was in the habit of writing to my aunts who lived far away, and today I realize that this was one of the ways I'd found to feel accepted and loved. My aunt Sue, who lived in California, would always find the time to write back, even though she was a single mom of three and had to work full-time! This meant a great deal to me! Also, my paternal grand-father would also write to me consistently until he passed away at the age of eighty-nine; I was twenty-one! He was one of my greatest losses!

Every so often, my mom would bring our cousins, Lorraine and Lucille, to play with us at home. We'd laugh so hard that we'd almost wet our pants, because Lorraine had a very funny sense of humour. One day, at the beach, she started telling me about the birds and the bees! I thought she was joking, as always. Finally she convinced me that one day I would have blood staining my underwear, which would mean that I was becoming a young woman as opposed to being a mere child. She reassured me by saying that all girls end up having the very same experience.

Two weeks before Christmas 1966, when I was at the tender age of twelve, blood stains appeared. I told my mom (who'd never spoken a word of this to either myself or my sister) and she quietly took out a sanitary napkin from the closet; it had a small belt, and she showed me how to use them;

because the napkin was so wide, I walked out of the washroom with my legs way far apart, as I did not want to squeeze the padding. My mom laughed when I asked her, "How am I supposed to walk with this apparatus in my pants?" She had no idea what to say.

My whole life was always one question after another; I wanted to know everything!

My dad was the one who attempted to answer them and when he could not, he would say, "That's a mystery; you'll know the answer 'if' you get to heaven."

Those good old religious mysteries always plugged the holes!

★　★　★

My mom often commented over the years that "Something's missing in [my] brain." Another one of her expressions, which she'd repeat over and over again when I did not want to do a chore, was, "OH! You won't die." Little did they know that I was missing the gene that causes a chemical imbalance in the brain and that I would eventually become mentally challenged. This is why I always had mood swings and was misunderstood by my parents, because I was very demanding; when I wanted something, I HAD to have it yesterday.

I was demanding, dramatic, an attention-seeker, was angry a lot of the time, and was a perfectionist; you name it, I had all of these characteristics which can possibly be found in some or many people who suffer from Bipolar illness.

M. L. CARMEN FORCIER

NOW IN JUNE OF 1967...

*I would like to explain that I consider prayer above all,
An act of gratitude for existence*

~Saul Bellow~

In June of 1967, my parents reluctantly decide to sell their dream home as there was a Canadian Tire store that had been built nearby after we moved there; every day, as my mom sat by her sewing machine, all she could see was a bunch of old tires at the back of the store, PLUS the noise from the car repair shop was almost deafening! My parents were quite heartbroken to leave this home, as our French church, which meant "all the gold in the world" to my mom, was only a block away, and the city buses stopped a quarter of a block from the house.

One sunny Sunday afternoon, we drove around as my parents were looking for homes that were for sale. One in particular had a sign that said "For Sale by Owner." We all got out of the car and were pleased with the environment, as the suburb called Riverside was, at that time, *the* finest area in which to live. My father negotiated the price within about one hour. We moved to our new surroundings about a month later. We were now living in our third home.

One month shy of my thirteenth birthday, it was in this home where I began teaching piano lessons to six students, for half an hour each every single week. My own lessons were now costing my mom four dollars per hour which allowed me to ask two dollars per hour from my own students.

Being quite well off (for those times) plus with all of my babysitting, I'd help my sister out once in a while, as my parents rarely gave her money. In those days, you went far with a twenty dollar bill.

★ ★ ★

One time, my sister asked my mom for three dollars. My mom asked her why she needed this certain amount. My sister answered by saying she needed to purchase nylon stockings. And so, off she went shopping with three dollars in hand. When she returned home, my dad was waiting!

HAVE NO FEAR; THERE HE STOOD WAITING FOR HER!

He asked what she had in her shopping bag; she had to reveal three or four small vinyl records. He flew into one of his tantrums. (my sister was no longer his preferred child—he'd abandoned his caring for her years before).

Seeing these records, and knowing she'd told my mom she was going to buy nylons, my father was so damn angry that he took the records from her hands and threw them towards a corner in the ceiling where they all fell to the floor into bits and pieces! His words were, "How dare you lie to your mother!"

CAN YOU JUST FEEL THAT LOVE?

AS FOR MYSELF...

Treasure your divinity

~M.L. Carmen Forcier~

I'd go shopping downtown almost every Saturday, discovering beautiful writing paper and greeting cards which I still love to this day! Occasionally I'd order clothing from the Eaton's catalogue. Also, I finally bought a few books of popular music. These I would play more often than my music homework.

Now, probably because we were forbidden to go to Detroit city, (across the river from Windsor), we'd go over on the bus with some friends. First off, we wore old clothes, because if we *did* buy any in Detroit, we would simply throw our worn clothes into a dumpster. Another funny thing is that we'd sometimes purchase three sets of clothing; we wore these coming back through the border. I'd never been questioned, though the guards had to know, because we were just bulging at the seams.

Once, I took this trip on my own, as dangerous as it was, having no fear whatsoever! YES—it was extremely dumb and very stupid of me!

WINDSOR WAS PREDOMINANTLY

I finally realized,
my task was not to figure out the one answer
but to learn how to live

~Marjorie Williams~

Windsor was predominantly an English-speaking city when I was growing up, although there were approximately 15,000 French-speaking Canadians then, many who'd come from the north of the province like my parents; others were from the provinces of Québec, New Brunswick, etc. There were no completely Francophone schools except for St. Edmonds, and another, mentioned below.

We therefore had our own French Canadian teachers in English Catholic schools. This situation remained so until I was in eighth grade, where I attended l'École Ste Rose, a totally French school. This was my last year, grade eight—before moving on to high school. At the end of the school year, my teacher chose me to be Valedictorian. I read a speech in front of all the student body, including their parents. What a great honour this was for me!

When I began ninth grade (high school) in the fall of 1968, my parents had a choice to send us to a Catholic Separate School and pay $500.00 per semester, or send us to George Vanier, a brand-new French-speaking high school where the Catholic religion was not taught, and there was no tuition fee. I was educated in the Separate School System (where Catholicism was taught) whereas my sister went to George Vanier for her last three years of high school.

★ ★ ★

As we became teenagers, my father would hide the clothes dryer fuses to prevent my sister from drying her jeans because she always took up too much electricity! He also stored a few cases of Coca-Cola AND toilet paper under lock and key! My sister broke these locks time and time again, though I never had the guts myself. When my dad would notice that some of these items were missing, we would both get a lecture; he never believed that my sister was the only one breaking into those cupboards. The fact that she had once been his favourite daughter was the reason most of the blame fell on me, as I was the eldest and should have been setting examples for my sister! And so the anger rose and kept rising for a very long time!

★ ★ ★.

Ever since I can remember, my dad and I were always at each other's throats! This went on and on every few days, for years and then some. Today I believe I now understand why! He never gave me reason to be right in any type of discussion! And so, for most of my life, having learned to argue, I remained clueless as how to have a normal, sane, human conversation.

The glory of friendship is not the outstretched hand,
nor the kindly smile, nor the joy of companionship.
It is the spiritual inspiration that comes to one, when one discovers
that someone else believes in him/her
and is willing to trust him/her.

~Ralph Waldo Emerson~

BEGINNING OF SUMMER, 1968

"Triumph" is just "umph" added to "try."

~Devotional book for Women~

At the beginning of the summer of 1968, my age was almost fourteen. I, along with my friend Pauline, were coming from my house, walking towards her high school. About halfway there, while standing on a corner, we met one of our friends called Pam's brothers, nicknamed "the tall one." Also standing with him was a guy by the name of John Lianzi, to whom Pauline introduced me.

I remember wearing a beautiful rainbow-coloured dress, my hair was a very dark brown and "Twiggy" short, and I was now making-up my eyes with liquid eyeliner and lots of mascara to show my long lashes. We both said hello to each other and it was love at first sight!

John was wearing khaki-coloured pants and a pale yellow short-sleeved shirt. What impressed me most about him was not only that he was very-good looking, and that he spoke in a very attractive thick English accent—he was also very funny!

Apparently, he and his sister (Angela) and their mom had just moved to our city of Windsor, from London, England. He mentioned that his father had been in the habit of beating his mom, so they came to Canada to escape his dad's angry temper. As we were being introduced, John kept making wisecracks and had us laughing within seconds. He'd given me a several quick winks; when the guys walked away, I'd found my first true love.

A few weeks went by, and one of my many friends called me to say there was a dance being held in a gym that night, in our neighbourhood, and was wondering if I would like to come. I said "Of course! I'd love to!"

Later that same evening, I was with about twenty or so of my friends. We were walking towards the dance hall; one of my friends by the name of David was accompanied by my friend Pam, his girlfriend. He said to me,

"Hey Carmen, you really caught John's attention the other day with your ever-so-long eyelashes!"

I was surprised to hear this, as I had not known the impression I had made on John. Upon entering the gym, there he was, keeping people in line to buy their tickets, speaking in that wonderful English accent of his! He noticed me and gave me one of his quick winks. I *knew* that he would become my boyfriend; the attraction was that strong!

One of our mutual friends, responsible for playing our songs with records we'd all brought in, had arranged speakers here and there around the gym. At around seven pm, we could hear The Beach Boys, The Rolling Stones, Pink Floyd, The Mamas and the Papas, etc.

John walked towards me and asked if I would dance with him. My heart soared! I'd never danced with a guy before! Guess what became our song?

We danced to The Beatles "Hey, Jude" which we all know does not really have an ending. It just keeps repeating "Na na na nana-na-na-na... hey, Jude..."

I'd had my arms around his neck, and he held me gently at the waist. We danced until someone finally stopped the record. I was so in love! John was a gentleman and knew how to make everyone laugh; he was the clown of our group AND he liked m*e!* I'd never felt so happy in my whole life! I was with the exact guy I wanted to be with; we felt strong emotions of happiness and love for each other!

ONE EVENING

The most powerful magnetic force in the universe
is the power of gratitude

~James Arthur Ray~

One evening...a few of our friends met up near a big tree. When it was time for me to go (I always had an early curfew!), I walked a ways with Pauline; she then went her way and I went mine, only I was scared to walk alone on this dark street.

So I walked back to the area where John, David, Wayne and a few others were sitting in the tree, talking away. Peeking through the branches, I asked if John could walk me home, saying it was quite dark. He eagerly agreed. I felt that this walk together would be the start of a deep relationship!

Throughout that summer and fall of 1968, John and I would see each other every time we met with our mutual friends, as well as every couple of days in the summer and every week or so once school started.

One day, we all met up in Pam's house, as she had to baby-sit her baby brother. We were all sitting in a large room (Pam had nine or ten siblings), feeling very happy to be together!

We'd heard through the grapevine that certain classes on discussions about religion were starting up for teenagers. They were going to be held in people's private homes. John and I began attending these meetings in search of answers to our questions, as these were the days when priests and nuns had started giving up their robes, their faith, etc. Religion was losing its respect from many types of people.

We were all a really good group of kids, feeling young and alive, in love and happy, and many of us paired off! Most of the time we'd get together just to hang out; on other occasions we'd go to the movies or had picnics with hot-dogs in the wooded areas nearby. Back then, if you had a boyfriend, it was because he'd asked you to "go around" with him.

Up until then, John had not asked me, although everyone knew we were very close!

I'd tell my parents the truth—that I was going to church meetings, in a family's private home, not too far away from where we lived. John would meet me halfway. He would gently put my head on his left shoulder while he had his left arm around my waist. We always walked together like this.

For me, it was a great comfort to know that John cared for me this much! He always made me feel deeply loved! As our first Christmas came along, he invited me to meet his mom and stepfather. I had just turned fourteen and John was almost eighteen. We were now at the end of 1968.

There we were, surrounded by our large group of friends, going into John's house, saying, "Merry Christmas! Hi, how are you? Hey, man! Hey, looking good! Cheers!"

John noticed my hair looked different and asked me what I had done, because he wanted me to make a really good impression on his parents. I said, "My mom curled it."

First, he introduced me to his stepfather, then his mom. This feeling of being embraced by loving people only happened with my friends, because at home, it was always dreary and depressing.

John had given me a box of chocolates, which I showed to my mom when I came home. Her stern response was that I was way too young to have a boyfriend. She also added with vehemence that I had to stop seeing him!

ONE DAY… ALL OF MY FRIENDS…

Kind words can be short and easy to speak,
but their echoes are truly endless

~Mother Teresa~

One day, all of my friends and I were able to purchase our own roller skates from our friend Janine's parents, as they owned a hardware store and were able to buy them at cost. When they arrived, I was so happy, because this meant that I no longer had to rent a pair every night we went skating.

As I walked into the front door with my box of skates, I took them out to show my dad. I was so proud, because he always looked for the cheapest things for anything he bought, and always calculated how to buy cases of carnation milk, soups, etc. for the lowest price.

I thought he'd be proud of me for having saved twenty-five dollars on a pair of skates that were regularly fifty dollars plus tax. Well, the first thing he said was, "You return those skates immediately!" in his very angry tone!

When I explained to him that I could not do so, he responded by saying that I could not have everything I wanted in life! This shocked me, as I'd always believed that I *could* have everything I desire!

(Prosperity consciousness had entered my brain at an early age.)

My mom would repeatedly say, "You're going to have to marry a doctor or a lawyer!"

He gave me an ultimatum: I would either return the skates, or he'd sell my precious bike. I had no choice.

The next day after school, while looking into the backyard, I asked my mom where my bike was (because I had not really believed that he would keep his word by punishing me so harshly). Her response was, "Your bike is gone—you should have listened to your father!"

Well, I continued roller-skating every day, though never did I own another bike until several years later!

AT THE AGE OF 14…

Ever tried. Ever failed. No matter.
Try again. Fail again. Fail better.

~Samuel Beckett~

At the age of fourteen, in 1968, my favourite subjects in school had always been literature/composition, both in French and English. I'd been an honour student for a few years and continued on this path until I reached grade twelve. I was constantly getting A+ in my English and French classes, and was writing really good essays, compositions, book reports, etc.

There was one teacher that I had while in ninth grade (my first year of high school) who taught English literature; his name was Mr. Johnson. While he was teaching at the front of the class, I would always be reading a book, never lifting my eyes, and never paying any attention to his lessons.

One day, this teacher caught one of my fellow students talking to another, and quickly sent him to the principal's office. A few minutes later, he saw Donald Lanthier giving a note to someone in the next row.

Well! That took the cake! Mr. Johnson asked Donald to also go to the principal's office for not paying attention to the lesson being taught.

Donald had been my boyfriend in grades four, five, and six, so we knew each other quite well. He sat right beside me, stood up and said, "Carmen here reads books every day in your classroom and you NEVER say a word of reproach to her!"

Hearing the conversation, I stood up and said, "Mr. Johnson, Donald is right; if you send him to the principal's office, I will accompany him."

The teacher reluctantly told us to sit back down. Class continued, and I went back to reading '*The biography of Vincent Van Gogh*' It was so sad that I silently wept at my desk.

Later on I learned he'd possibly been BIPOLAR; furthermore, among the geniuses of music composers from centuries past, many may have suffered from this same mental illness.

REMEMBERING...
REMINISCING

OUR GREATEST MOMENTS WERE...

Ignorance on fire is better than knowledge on ice.

~Unknown~

Our greatest moments were when we roller - skated from April to October. We would rent the boot skates, the ones with four wheels, and then go 'round and 'round the arena, which hardly had any air to breathe—it was SO HOT in there.

I was about thirteen, and my sister was eleven when we first started—so this was from 1967 to 1971. Of course, we were there to be seen with our dark tans by the guys. When they had couples only, we often sat through those moments. Our chances were better when it was triplets only. We'd of course be the middle person with two guys on each side, holding on for dear life. Let me tell you, when we rounded the corners, we were speeding so fast it felt like we were flying; luckily we never encountered any falls.

After a while, some guys would ask us to skate, having spotted us from the bleachers. A couple of years later, while going to the arena eight nights a week, a guy named Paul Bilorosik asked me, "Hey kiddo, 'wanna' skate?" while it was couples only! Wow! Was I ever happy! He was also kind of cute. For a few months thereafter, we'd meet and skate, enjoying each other's company.

Burger King had just opened a franchise, and was always the place to go afterwards to hang out with quite a few other roller skaters; the price for a Whopper and fries with small drink was ninety-five whole cents! We all could afford this.

My parents never knew about our going into cars with guys. We felt pretty good about this, as we were so often limited to feel any joy. My mother still maintains to this day that one is not allowed to feel joy on this earth; only when you go to heaven can you allow yourself any kind of happiness—that is, if you make it there at all...'cause it's really hard to get into that place!

NOW IN GRADE 10...

Nothing valuable can be lost by taking time.

~Abraham Lincoln~

In grade ten, I was age fifteen. It was September 15, 1969, and I'd forgotten my gym shoes in the locker room the previous week. I went to the head office of my high school to ask if anyone had seen or found my runners. They looked around, but did not find any blue shoes. So I went to my gym class, barefoot, without even a pair of socks.

At one point, my left foot, because it was a little sweaty, jammed and twisted on itself. Oh my goodness, it hurt! As I was holding my leg up to ease the pain, one of my classmates said, "Holy Mother of God! Carmen, what did you do?"

The expression on her face was one of devastation. Apparently, my left foot was facing away from my ankle at 180 degrees! The principal was immediately called into the gym and asked me for my home phone number. I said, "Do I really have to tell you?" I was desperate! Theres no way I wanted my parents to find this out as I would never hear the end of it, and they'd be so angry with me!

Anyways, after giving my home number, an ambulance arrived at the back of the school; the attendants came straight in to examine me. Well, first off, they said I could not hold my left leg up as this was preventing the blood from circulating towards my foot. Geepers! It hurt so much when they took my leg down and tied it on the sheet of a small gurney. As they wheeled me out, the whole school was watching, and there was a buzz everywhere.

"What happened? Who is she? What's going on?"

As I approached the ambulance, someone cried out, having recognized me, and said, "Carmen has been injured!"

Upon arriving at the hospital, x-rays were taken straight away. I was left alone for three hours in the hallway, in EXTREME PAIN, but I smiled at everyone who walked by, though no one seemed to notice!

The orthopaedic specialist finally arrived. As I was being wheeled into a nearby room, the doctor was studying my x–rays; ALL OF A SUDDEN, he grabbed my left foot in his right hand and cracked my ankle back into place.

I immediately sat up and said, WHOA! Why did you not tell me you were going to do that?"

His response was, "It hurts less when a patient does not expect pain to occur." HOLY SMOKES! His next words were, "No eating or drinking. You are booked to be in an O.R. for eight pm."YIKES!

My thoughts were, *I'm so darn thirsty and have not eaten since eight this morning.* It was ten am upon my entering emergency; the time now was one pm; eight pm was a very long ways away! UN-BE-LIE-VA-BLE!

Finally, I was taken to a four-bed room. (My family doctor had seen me upon my arrival.) There I lay, waiting. At one point, my gym teacher came to see me to say how sorry she was. I felt very grateful for this!

THEN, BOOM! in came my mom, at around two-thirty pm. She started giving me shit for having disturbed her routine, telling me that she had no time for this, and that she could not stay because she had to go home to cut someone's hair!

I was TOTALLY RELIEVED that she'd gone as fast as she'd arrived, because her attitude was one that I really, really did not need!

Now, you have to be aware that when you go to the O.R., the rules say that you MUST remove your nail polish, jewellery and especially your make-up. I begged and begged my doctor to let me keep my eye make-up on, as no one had ever seen me look plain since I'd had my eyelashes grown back in. I SIMPLY HAD TO maintain my "Maybelline Image." Finally, he relented and let me keep my face looking just the way I wanted.

He continued by explaining how my injury was a clean break of both big bones on either side of my left ankle. They were to insert a metal PIN in the inside bone, which in turn would help both sides to heal.

(Apparently, during my operation, nurses were convinced my lashes were fake! My GP assured them they were quite real!)

When I woke up, I saw my cast. It went from the left hip to just above my toes. They were the only visible part of my left leg! Luckily, I could move them; they were warm to touch and pink in colour.

Of course, they had to place a urinal catheter during the operation. There it was…filling with very little yellow fluid. Finally, a nurse gave me some ice chips to suck on. That was the best thing that had happened to me all day! What a relief to be able to wet the inside of my mouth!

Shortly afterwards, another nurse brought me a sandwich and a small drink, which I had to eat and sip slowly to prevent any vomiting.

One of my visiting friends in hospital had heard from the head office at school that they'd apparently found my runners! Is this not the darnedest thing?

ONE DAY…PAUL MOVED…

*Sometimes we are so busy adding up our troubles
that we forget to count our blessings.*

~Devotional book for Women~

One day, Paul moved from Windsor to London, Ontario to attend university. The next time I saw him was when I was in hospital with my big cast and all. He'd wanted to take me out although he was happy to visit me every day for a week or so.

Nearing Christmastime, at the end of his university semester, he came over to my house and gave me a gift of very expensive leather gloves. Of course they did not fit; so off we went to the store where he'd bought them and made the exchange. I begged and begged my mom to have him stay for dinner although her answers were always an outright flat "NO!"

Not long after the holidays, Paul invited me to a party one of his friends was giving; I said "YES!" instantly. When he came to pick me up, my dad had insisted that Paul ask his permission to attend this party. Of course, the good old early curfew still applied!

While sitting on a sofa surrounded by a lot of teenagers, Paul coughed and at the same time put his arm around me over the back of the sofa. I thought that was so cute as he'd always been somewhat shy. Once he'd mentioned taking me to a sort of prom and that we'd be married after I met his family.

A few months later, his friend told me Paul was going out with a whole lot of girls at his university in London, Ontario; the suggestion was to forget him altogether, which I did.

ON ANOTHER OCCASION...

If you look at the cost of life, you have poverty consciousness;
if you look at the value of life you will create abundance.

~Bob Proctor~

On another occasion, a guy, previously unknown to me, asked me to skate, and so we did, for the whole evening. When we walked out of the arena, I hesitated to get into his car. He kept asking me questions on what I liked to do, how I felt about this, what was my opinion on that, on and on! We must have talked for over an hour. He even asked me if he could drive me home.

As I felt no fear, I said, "OK."

Once in front of my house, he kept asking more questions; I thought, "*Well, maybe this guy has seen me around and really likes me!*" It was a few weeks before I encountered him again.

(There's a really good twist to this story!—you have to follow what I'm going to say very carefully, because at this time, my age was sixteen, and I'd left home.)

This story is about a guy named David Ferris.

Walking down my street, a few houses away and across the street, there was that same guy, bent forward looking like he was fixing his car. I said hello;

he did not look surprised to see me. We had a short conversation. Then I continued on my walk.

His car was parked in front of David Ferris' house and I kind of figured they were very good friends.

One of my girlfriends who lived exactly across the street from David had the worst crush on him as he was the biggest HUNK around. She would move the curtain, watching him when he left and returned back home. Once, I noticed he'd kind of stared back at her from his driveway; this alone convinced her David also had a crush on HER.

My friends and I would often go to football games when our school was playing. On one occasion, as we were filing out of the bleachers, moving toward the bottom, my friend Pauline asked me to look up at the top of the bleachers only to see David Ferris staring right at me. I felt his gaze instantly, for it was quite intense. I thought to myself… *WOW! If only I could go out with THIS GUY…I'd be in seventh heaven!* He was blond and probably blue-eyed as well.

As my mom was known in the neighbourhood as a "home" hairdresser, David's mom had come over a few times. She would talk to me and ask me questions; I mean, I hardly knew her and had never really seen or met her before!

She came back a second time, a few months later. Apparently their faith was that of the Jehovah Witnesses and she must have caught on that my mother was an "EXTREMELY DEVOUT CATHOLIC!"

Time passed. One day, my sister, being fourteen, had gone bowling with some of her friends and guess who she saw looking at her? Yep! Sure enough, it was the HUNK, David Ferris, the guy every girl wanted to go out with!

After they talked a while, he drove her home, and apparently they went on dates from that moment on, for a couple of months.

One evening, he asked her to dinner in his own home as his parents were going to be out for a while. She went to his place and they had a wonderful time together. My sister had kept this whole story from me for years!

As she started her story, I was shocked to hear they'd been dating 'cause this guy was way too old for her—like eighteen or nineteen.

She finally got to the part about the dinner they had at his house and how they were French kissing that night! HUH? All of a sudden, he'd stopped and said he had to tell her something very important.

Take a wild guess as to what happened next!

His very words were the following: "The only reason I went out with you is because I've always had this huge crush on your sister, Carmen, and was hoping I'd get to meet her if ever I went to your house." He added the following thought, "The truth is, I've always wanted to ask your sister Carmen to go out with me and be my girl!"

The end! She never saw him again. Meanwhile, back at the ranch, I was exploding with such disappointment! All the years we'd lived down the street from each other, he'd had a crush on *moi?* The last thing he said to my sister was, "I was so scared to ask your sister out on a date, because I definitely always thought she would say no!"

GO FIGURE, EH? I would have been the envy of every girl had he asked me that simple question!

Remember my second encounter with David's friend while fixing his car in front of Davids house. The evening we had met, he and I had talked so much; he seemed sincerely interested in me and wanted to know as much about me as he possibly could. Turns out David had asked him to get to know me better!

WOW! I could hardly believe this far-fetched story! Then I remembered David's mom coming to my house to get her hair done, and the way she'd been so interested in me; everything became clear!

AT ABOUT THIS SAME TIME...

Tis friends and not places that make the world

~Bliss Carmen~

At about this same time, I saw Jocy for the second time. She was so BEAUTIFUL! We both recognized each other straight away, and I was so very happy to see her! She was so full of love! We spent the rest of the day AND night, catching up on the latest news. I felt so close to her and admired her so much—she was the most loving person I had ever met.

In June of 1970, I was fifteen years old, and I started writing poetry. Jocy was always amazed at my writing skills. She eventually became the person to whom I would send my writings; she's always told me how she loves my rhymes. Her constant encouragement over many years was very generous and uplifting.

She ALWAYS made me feel so validated! Her recognition of my work meant everything to me.

AS THE YEARS WENT BY...

I realised happiness is a by-product of curiosity and surrender, not of pursuit and entitlement.

~Gretel Ehrlich~

As the years went by, tension mounted in our home by a hundredfold. For example, on Christmas Day, 1968, my aunts and uncles were visiting in our partly-finished basement, and my cousins and I were upstairs. The phone rang, and when I answered, it was John. He was having a party and wanted me to come over and celebrate with all of our friends.

I had heard someone on the other phone we had downstairs, as I could hear the family talking in the background. Darn it—it was icy outside and my boots were in a room in the basement! I had to go downstairs to get them, and then my cousin Richard and I were going to walk to John's home to join the party, and introduce him to my friends.

As I was going back up the stairs with my boots in hand, my mother yelled at me and said: "Where are you going with those?" My answer was that Richard and I were going to see my friends at John's house as they were having a get-together to celebrate Christmas.

Well, in her "off-the-wall reaction" she said, "You're not going anywhere to see John or any of your friends! I heard you on the phone a few minutes ago; you're not going 'parking'!"

I said, "It's a *party,* and John's parents are chaperoning…I'm not going 'parking' with anyone!"

You see, because of John's English accent, my mom had heard the word "parking" instead of "party" and so both my parents were furious—so angry, in fact, that they actually asked every relative to go home, as they had to "deal" with me, their daughter!

I saw my mom's family leaving through the living room door, giving me sideway glances of disapproval. I then went to the washroom, locked the door, and cried. I felt so rejected from all sides! Both my broken heart and humiliation were absolutely crushing!

Now came the REAL trouble. It was only ten pm. My father raised his voice (surprise?) and ordered me out of the washroom to come join my family in the living room (some family!). Would you believe that from ten pm to one am, my father raged at me, on and on and on, non-stop, repeating that I was too young to have a boyfriend, asking, "How could you even *think* of going 'parking?'"

I could not fit in two words to defend myself, nor give any explanation that all of my girlfriends had boyfriends and that their parents accepted this as normal behaviour. I actually cried for the full three hours of lecturing and then some after going to bed.

This was the first time he threatened to send me to a convent if I did not stop seeing John. Well, that scared me to death. I would have been sent away to an all-girls school, away from everyone I loved, and would have been isolated for about four years, until I at least finished high school!

Although I was very frightened by this predicament, and terrified of my father, I had no intention of breaking up with John. I had learned to have a few guts of my own.

TIME PASSED....

To be the greatest, be a servant

~Matthew 23:11 (TLB)~

My parents went to my grand-parents' house for New Year's Day. My sister and I chose not to go. As soon as they were out of sight, I called my friend Pamela and asked her to phone everyone to have them come to my house, as my parents would be out for a while. Within a half-hour, my friends were all there, calling me mother superior kneeling on the floor for me to bless them all. This became my nickname due to the convent threat! While the others were all downstairs, we sat upstairs in the living room, and John's head rested on my lap. Admiring the beautiful Christmas tree, he suddenly said, "Would you go around with me?" Thrilled that he did not fear my father, my answer was a definite "YES!"

We walked to the basement stairs and announced to everyone that we were now officially "going around." Everyone laughed and said they'd known that for a long time. It was funny and also a great feeling to know that I still had my support team even though my dad was SO mean and my mom SO strict!

John and I went back upstairs for some quiet time (no kissing!) Then, out of the blue, my parents' car was coming up the driveway! They'd only been gone maybe ninety minutes or so. I panicked and ran downstairs to tell my friends they had to go immediately as my parents were home!

They all ran out the back door as my parents entered the front door! I was practically pushing them out. They climbed our fenced yard, walking quickly into the field beyond, trying not to leave any trace of having been at my house.

However, I did notice my father looking out at the field from the kitchen window, watching a bunch of teenagers running for their lives. I'm pretty sure he knew they'd been in the house, although he could not prove it. Whew! That was a close call! Man, was I EVER SCARED to go to that convent!

A few days later, my father came out with another one of his brilliant ideas. He threatened me by saying that if any of his own friends saw me with John—*anywhere*—he would immediately arrange for my convent days to begin.

John and I kept meeting each other twice a week, through the religious groups in people's homes, and he'd always hold my hand whenever he had the opportunity. If my curfew was ten pm and we still had an hour or so before I was due back home, we would walk the streets of our neighbourhood, with my head always on his left shoulder and his left arm always around my waist. We just wanted to be together all the time; this was very comforting for us both. It was now the middle of winter; no matter how cold it was, we'd walk around hugging each other while the snow fell, until it was time for me to go home.

On one of those nights, I saw a car that looked exactly like my dad's, riding around the streets. I knew he was looking for me, trying to catch John and I together, so that he could have some proof that I was disobeying his orders. John and I kept walking for another forty-five minutes or so, and my dad always seemed to miss us by a few blocks—maybe so we'd feel threatened? We were being followed—and it's not like we were somewhere hiding, kissing and hugging. It was not like that! We simply wanted to be together!

As I came home that night, my dad was just pulling into the driveway with the dirtiest look on his face, asking where I'd been. I said, "To a church meeting with my friends." I was home on time, having always observed most of my curfews! He apparently had not seen us walking about!

MY PARENTS HARDLY EVER SPOKE...

Men never do evil so completely and cheerfully as when they do it from a religious conviction.

~Blaise Pascal~

My parents hardly ever spoke to each other unless my mom was saying to my dad what she wanted at the grocery store (every Saturday afternoon). After dinner, both my parents read parts of the newspaper while my sister and I did the dishes. My mom never talked to my sister and I unless it was to yell, criticize, or punish us—most of which we never understood!

She was constantly being the at-home hairdresser, running up and down the stairs to the basement, sewing clothes or doing crafts. She taught both my sister and I how to make our own clothes, though during these times, there were huge arguments; either my sister would tell my mom "where to go" or I would become impatient and insist my clothes be sewn perfectly, not wanting to be like my mom, sewing this way and that, never finishing a piece of clothing properly.

Her Catholic religion taught her to never care for the beauty of our earth. She was indifferent towards anything and everything imaginatively pretty. To this day, if my mom allows herself to feel any joy, happiness, relief, or has a feeling of well-being at all, she immediately goes to confession to wash away her sins for having felt well inside! Another point I'd like to make here is that she cannot even stand to watch anyone else experiencing any kind of happiness. Now that's just plain sick, if you ask me!

Briefly...

Whenever we went shopping for paper patterns to sew our clothes, my mom would always choose size fourteen for me and size twelve for my sister. What was the reason for this? Well, if my sister and I had known we had much slimmer bodies, it would have been considered a mortal sin to even have those thoughts because this was all connected to the terrible word *sex*. Now get this—every time she worked with a pattern, she would pin the whole paper pattern around our bodies, and adjust them accordingly because they never did fit us! Why, you may wonder; sexy feelings? Turns out, my sister was a size two and I, a size nine!

Go figure!

WE WERE NEVER ALLOWED...

Ask the universe, "How may I serve?"
Its response to me will be,
"How may I serve you?"

~Wayne Dyer~

We were never allowed to laugh at the dinner table. Once, in our third home, when my sister and were teenagers, we (for some unknown reason) broke out laughing. Then we suddenly stopped, as we were terrified of my dad. We tried our best to not even smile. Then, as my mouth was full of peaches, I just cracked up, unable to keep my laughter inside. My mouth opened wide and there went the juice from my mouth right into my dad's face! Oh, my God! He was FURIOUS to say the least.

Immediately, he roared out, "Stop this nonsense at once!"

Gizèle and I walked away from the dinner table and went to the washroom where we usually went after a meal. We would always find something to laugh about; here was a place our dad could not enter while we were in this room, although he would often bang on the door and tell us we'd been in there too long; he would demand that we get out—there were others who needed the facilities!

Our having fun drove him nuts. He never could stand either of us crying or laughing; he just did not have the nerves to hear either sadness or joy!

We walked out, and since I was used to butting heads with my dad, my next words to him were, "Yes, but when you're in the washroom, you sit there and read for more than a half-hour, every single time." In other words, we also had a right to stay in the washroom for as long as he did.

This was not a pretty scene! He was so angry that we left very quickly in order to avoid another family fight.

Ten minutes passed. Gizèle and I were cleaning the dishes. My father walked up to us and said, "I want you to promise me you'll never laugh out loud at the table while we're eating, ever again, or else I'm going to punish you for this evening!"

My sister immediately made the promise, although I chose not to. No frigging way was I going to cave into his usual traps, because I knew I would not be able to keep this promise.

My dad looked at me with his usual angry face and was just steaming as I'd had the nerve to take the punishment instead of expressing my apologies. He was not prepared for my reaction! Standing there, he yelled out, "Do not play games with me! I'll find some kind of punishment for you, just you wait!"

I was always proud of myself whenever I could tick him off, as that was the way I got my revenge AND satisfaction from his sick and twisted manipulative mind.

Ten minutes later, my dad came back to the kitchen uttering my punishment. He said that I could not watch any TV shows for one whole week, that I was to read in my parents' room. WOW, if he only knew how easy that was for me. Reading was and still is one of my greatest passions!

When my week began, I went to their bedroom with a good book, and for seven days, I mostly read!

Now, my mom and I had been following the soap *Peyton Place* after dinner. During this reading period of mine, I'd often go to the washroom across the hall to get a good view of the living room where I could get great glimpses of the soap to keep up with with the story. So really, I never felt

I'd been given a punishment! This made me feel that I'd won at least one battle with my dad! Yeah!

EVEN THOUGH WE'D MOVED...

Falsehood has an infinity of combinations
but truth has only one mode of being.

~Jean Jacques Rousseau~

Even though we'd moved to our third house, I still continued taking piano lessons from the same teacher, which meant that I had to take three buses there and three more to come back home. Fortunately, my lessons were on Saturdays.

Now on the third bus back, I would take another route so that John and I could meet up and walk a ways together. On this one big corner where my last bus turned, I would first get off to see if John and a few friends were having fries in the K-Mart store. Sometimes they were, although most times no one was there. When that was the case, I would just walk down the long street towards my home and very often met John on my way, walking towards me with his big black dog.

He would always show up somewhere along this road around the time I was due to pass so that we could steal precious moments of our lives talking, and to just *be* together. He was always faithfully there to meet me every Saturday.

On one of those days, a certain car went by and honked at us. Recognizing it to be one of my parents' friends, I remembered my dad's threat to send me away to the convent if ever he heard from anyone he knew that they'd seen me with a guy. I was really scared!

Dearest John, we loved each other so much!

One day, in late January 1969, when I was still aged fourteen, my dad was leaving home to work an extra shift, and my mom was out. I got a brilliant idea—I sneaked down to the basement to use the phone, and called John to let him know that I could walk to his house, as my parents would be out. He said he was free, and that his parents were out as well. I'd JUST put the receiver down without making a sound.

My dad appeared at the head of the stairs, just checking to see if I was up to something! WHEW! Close call! So, he went on his way and I hurried to get dressed. Wanting to spend as much time as I could with John, I walked briskly through the snow to save some time, arriving at his home within twenty minutes or so.

You've got to keep in mind that I would never let John kiss me—ever! Once during the previous fall, while walking me home, he'd pecked me with a kiss; I was shocked—it did not feel like a sin at all, like my mom said it would. It was the simplest of gestures and his lips felt soft and warm.

OK, so now we were both in his home, alone, just the two of us. John showed me around the house; when I saw that he only had a single bed in his own room, I said, "I thought you had a double bed!" as he'd always joked about that. He just grinned and then led me to the living room sofa, where we both sat down close together. You have to remember that he was almost eighteen years of age and I was only fourteen!

He started kissing me. All of a sudden, I asked, "Could you please pull the curtains shut?" as I was always suspicious of people watching my every move, because my mom would always say, "What would people think if..." Both my sister and I would always feel like we were being watched while walking the streets, anywhere!

Now, no one could see us. We start kissing and it felt really nice! This was our first time alone together, ever. I trusted him completely. After a few moments, he French kissed me! Well, you should have seen me jump!

M. L. CARMEN FORCIER

I immediately got up from the sofa and ran to the room where he'd put my coat and things. I was just boiling with anger—and I mean *boiling,* because my mom had said that French kissing was a sin; I certainly was already *so* fearful of going to hell that I could not accept this gesture of affection from the one I loved. There was a mirror in the room, and unfortunately, I saw my angry face and felt so ashamed!

All my friends kissed and made out, but not me, the so-called "saint" or "Mother Superior." John came running after me; I explained to him what was going on in my head and he kept saying, "Just come back to the living room and I promise I will not French kiss you again!" but my anger was so visible and loud!

I placed my scarf around my neck and put on my coat, and right out of the blue John dropped to his knees facing me, with both hands together as in prayer, and begged and begged me to forgive him!

Gosh! I felt like such an absolute fool, loser, and idiot. There he was, asking me to spend the afternoon with him, and I decided, *No I have to go home!* But of course, I forgave him right away.

He must have really cared for me. I often think of those precious moments, during which I was so angry and fearing the fires of eternal hell. He'd taken the time to calm me down, understanding how wicked my parents were.

He then walked me most of the way back home.

ONE EVENING, MID-JANUARY...

The best bridge between hope and despair
is often a good night's sleep.

~Devotional book for Women~

One evening, in mid-January, John and our mutual friend Michael (who was black) came to pick me up to go ice-skating. Approaching the kitchen after hearing the doorbell, I heard my mom yell out, "You get out of my house! We do not allow black people in our home!"

She threw Michael out into the winter snow and cold while John stood at the kitchen sink waiting for me to get ready. Upon my arrival at the scene, I quickly realized the situation and felt SO embarrassed. It was freezing outside! My mom said that Negroes were not allowed to live in our neighbourhood.

She then screamed at John, in a wild wicked witch's pitch, "Are you ca-to-lic? Do you talk French?"

His response was, "No, I am a protestant, born in England, and do not speak French."

My mom then started yelling at him, saying that I was way too young to have a boyfriend, and to get the hell out of her house. Meanwhile, my dad stood nearby, smoking away, tense as a post, also angry as hell. I was SO humiliated that I just took my coat, and we were out of there within minutes! My life was becoming a nightmare!

★ ★ ★

Not too long after this, my mom and sister were out for the evening. My father was in the washroom and heard me knock on the door. He said to wait a few moments. So, I stood outside the door, leaning against a wall.

Finally, my dad walked out, and immediately slapped me REALLY HARD on my right cheek, with the back of his huge left hand—KA-FLOW!

My head went back, banged on the wall, and I was soon slipping to the floor. I managed to get myself back up before falling completely, but I was absolutely SHOCKED out of my brain!

Holding my cheek with my right hand, I stared at my dad who was now standing in his bedroom, smoking away, looking at me with the fiercest eyes.

He then said, "This will teach you to never ever dare bring into this house any kind of BLACK person—or BROWN person, for that matter!"

As my stare met his, I said, "Love one another as I have loved you!"

He looked at me with such a cruel expression I truly felt he was going to kill me! Honest to God!

Never did I speak a word of this to anyone until I was thirty-five. I finally did speak of it in 1989, when I was telling our minister.

She commented, "It only takes one time!"

THE FOLLOWING FEBRUARY...

Broken hearts, torn dreams
Open hearts, mended dreams.

~Anthony Robbins~

The following February, I asked my mom if I could have a party in the finished basement room. She was not thrilled at the idea and I had to '*really*' beg for her approval. After about three days, she and my dad finally agreed!

I was going to set the room up so that everyone coming would have something to sit on. I promised my parents that the day after the party, two of my friends would come help me to clean up and re-arrange the furniture back to its original place.

Once again, I called my friend Pam to help me spread the word to all of our friends so that they were made aware of the date and time of the party. Pam was always the one who contacted the others as she had everyone's phone number.

On that particular Saturday night in mid–April, the whole group came—all except for John, of course, as he was banned to even come near my house. My dad was working the evening shift and my mom sat at the top of the stairs in the kitchen, listening to everything we were saying.

Now hear this!

Every single time we all got up to slow dance, my mom would come charging downstairs, physically separating each couple (with her rough hands), expressing her distress to all of us who were clinging to each other. She would turn all the lights back on, giving us a religious lecture on how sex was a really big sin and that dancing that way was just attracting the devil to ourselves. She would then resume her place at the top of the stairs. This went on all evening—back and forth, up and down!

She'd always made it her mission to show herself as being superior to others, TRULY believing she had a duty to the world; her duty was to show how disrespectful people were to each other AND towards God! She was always full of hatred while representing herself as a being a REAL Christian.

By ten-thirty pm, my dad was home from work. In all her anger, my mom explained to him what she'd been through all evening and how we had all so misbehaved!

That was it! My dad came halfway downstairs and said, "All of you people GET OUT NOW!"

It was not a pretty picture. Everyone streamed out of the house within five minutes, scared to death, all of them reassuring me that they were still my friends. Some kissed me on the forehead, saying not to worry!

★ ★ ★

Later, in 1984, my oncle Jean passed away, and she declared to her family (being quite sure of herself) that SHE was sending him to 'limbo' because he did not deserve to see God or be in heaven, as he'd always made fun of religion!

★ ★ ★

The next morning, I woke up depressed, and had not slept very well. My mother had said that I would NEVER again have another party! The two friends who were coming to help me clean the previous night's party scene were a little late, so I decided to start putting things back in order myself.

My father called me to his workshop and was so utterly pleased with himself. He smugly said, "You see, you have no real friends; no one came to help you!"

I went back to my duties, and within another fifteen minutes, both my friends arrived to help me.

But wait! There's more—as if anything worse could happen.

My mom asked the three of us to stand in the kitchen while my dad stood a few feet away in the living room (so as to hear the lecture she was about to give us) smoking away his darn cigarettes, just making sure my mom got her pressing message across.

My mom was standing, leaning on the kitchen counter, staring at us with such vengeance that I said to myself, *OH boy! Now what?* As she started her demeaning speech, and while pointing her finger at all three of us, she said:

"The way you were dancing last night is a mortal sin! You'll have to go to confession to ask a priest to pardon you and then recite your penance, asking God for forgiveness…because when God created Adam and Eve, he gave them his whole paradise. But, you see, God's REAL PLAN was that man would reproduce himself in a special way, and not through the sinful act of sex."

According to my mom, God had another plan for man to pro-create and was punishing all of humanity through the act of sex. God chased Adam and Eve out of his paradise, telling them they would now lead a life of sin, labour, hard work, and suffering for having eaten the forbidden fruit!

By this time, she was unable to look at us; she had her head bent down, and was crying crocodile tears. Immediately, I hugged her, feeling very sorry for her, trying to console her—although what could I say? I did not believe in this stuff!

I put my arms around her neck, feeling *so* mortified. She spoke as though she were God's personal messenger on earth.

Over the years, she's become THE most self-righteous person I've ever met! She's only gotten meaner over the years. My dad always said that she reads religious articles only!

There is one book she did read, and that was the Von Trapp family story. On a few occasions, she would sit in the living room with a huge bible on her lap and read from the Old Testament, not understanding a word I'm sure, as she hardly had any education—though to her, this action (she believed) would give her much better chances, to enter heaven on the day she met with her creator.

It gets even better!

FEELING SO DEPRESSED...

Worry is like a rocking chair:
it gives you something to do,
but doesn't get you anywhere.

~Devotional book for Women~

I just really, *really* wanted to die! HONESTLY! A few hours later, the phone rang and it was for *moi*. I picked up the receiver, expecting absolutely nothing, as I was *so* down. Then I heard Pam's voice asking me how I was feeling (by this time, all of my friends had heard of my mom's speech).

I was so glad to hear Pam's sympathetic voice. Then another one of my friends, Pauline, spoke and asked me the same question. It was so nice to hear from them and I could sense some laughter in the background, but thought nothing of it.

Then, out of the blue, Pauline said, "Do you want to speak with Sally?" My response was, "Who in the world is Sally?"

She kept repeating that "Sally" wanted to ask me a question. None of us had any friend called Sally, so I was totally confused! All of a sudden, I heard a familiar voice—and to my greatest surprise, it was John!

He said, "Hi, this is Sally!"

I said, "Oh! Sally! SALLY! Hi, how are you? It's been a while since we last saw each other!"

I'd never been happier to hear his comforting voice and English accent! OH! Man! Was I ever happy!

Once he realized I'd guessed their little game, to surprise me, he asked me if I wanted to go to the movies with him and a few of our friends. I froze, because I'd just been grounded for two weeks. Nonetheless, Pauline and Jeanine, the two friends who'd come to help me clean up after the party, were on their way over.

An hour later, we were all ecstatic! They explained to my mom that we were just going to the movies with "Sally" and a few other girls.

Finally, my mom relented, though she insisted I be home at nine-thirty pm, which was really early AND a punishment at the same time, for the movie started at around seven-thirty pm.

So we took off and walked to the corner where we met the others. Fantastic! We had pulled it off! John came up to me and took my hand in his; we were so happy to see each other!

We had a great time on the bus going downtown, and found good seats in the theatre, with most of us sitting in couples. The title of the movie was '*Bullet*' with Steve McQueen. It was fantastic!

Afterwards, the cinema was showing a special short documentary on England, and John REALLY wanted to see his homeland. Meanwhile, the clock was ticking, and I was running out of time to arrive home at nine-thirty pm. I nudged him reluctantly a few times, asking him, "Can we please leave?" because I was *so* afraid of disobeying my parents, convent and all!

He finally stood up, although not in the best of moods. We all knew my parents never allowed enough time for me to reach home within the time frames they dictated to me. As we caught the bus home, we sat together, although John was not talking to me; this was extremely difficult and made me VERY sad.

We'd never had a fight, and I only knew our loving times. When we arrived at my stop, we started walking down my street, but you know, he was not

M. L. CARMEN FORCIER

holding my hand, so I really *knew* and *felt* how upset he was. I felt really down and disappointed, and the anger towards my parents was increasing by the minute!

As we neared one block from my house, John said, "You can walk the rest of the way home by yourself," in a very pissed-off tone. He said good night and was on his own way home, by himself also, as most of our friends were still at the cinema.

I got home later than promised, no questions asked.

NEARING THE END
OF MARCH/1969

*We are each of us angels with one wing,
and can only fly embracing one another.*

~Luciano de Crescenzo~

Nearing the end of March, 1969, I was still fourteen years old—and the worst thing in my life happened!

I'd just gotten off the bus from my music lessons, meeting John (as we always did on Saturdays). After walking and talking for a while, and just before we went our separate ways, he stopped and said, "I think it's a good idea if we break up and let things cool down for a while."

THE worst moment in my life!

I said, "For how long?" My brain was shocked to the max!

He then said, "It's only for three months."

Confirming his words, my question was, "So in three months time, we'll be back together again, RIGHT?"

He assured me, "Yes, that's RIGHT."

As broken-hearted as I was, I trusted him, and also recognised what kind of pressure we were always under, due to my parents.

As we parted, with both of us looking over our shoulders, we waved back to each other!

IN JUNE OF 1970...

*How far does the human heart
have to travel to peace?*

~Denis Kucinich~

When I was fifteen years old, I wrote my very first poem. The following thoughts you see below came into my head so fast, I could hardly keep up with the thoughts from my brain to my hand! This may also be a warning a sign of being BIPOLAR, having racing thoughts, often accompanied by HIGHS and swift heart palpitations. This is when one should seek immediate medical attention.

Written June 9th and 10th, 1970 (Thursday/ Friday)

WHAT LIFE IS TO ME!

Somewhere lays a newborn baby...
The sun is bright yet somewhat hazy
His heart is beating, his skin so soft
The water splashes on the sand and rocks.

To hold him close, to see him smile
The wind keeps blowing all the while.
His face is innocent, he says not a word
Not far away, a church bell is heard.

He stops, he listens, he cries again
"Go in peace," says the priest, "Mass is at end."
His hunger satisfied, his stomach content
A new day has come, life's no longer silent.

His eyes are now open, looking with wonder
A dog is heard barking there over yonder.
An image, a face, she's special, he knows
Traffic is heavy on the main roads.

In the name of the Father, name of the Son
Children play, laugh and run.
The stain on his soul is gone forever
A mailman walks briskly delivering a letter.

He tries to walk, goes forward a few steps
An old man is worried about paying his debts.
He babbles a word that sounds like "Mum"
A soldier is killed by an enemy gun.

He asks many questions, discovers new things
Flowers to his loved one, a young man brings.
Many years have gone by, he's going to school
They say PEACE should be the golden rule.

His heart is always filled with happiness and love
While lonely souls pray, asking help from above.
He sees not any sorrow, feels not any pain
In darkness walks a woman with her white cane.

Now he's growing up things aren't the same
He sees it all around him, the world is insane.
"Why," he asks, "is there such misery?
Can't we all live in peace and harmony?"

Hunger and death, he has seen many times
A new child is born, so innocent his mind.
Eighty years of life, he has learned to be wise
He pities the soul not yet baptized.

M. L. CARMEN FORCIER

His skin is now wrinkled, not soft any more
Jealousy and hatred are the causes of war.
His heart is much weaker, his time has now come
The sun is now seeping through the horizon.

~M.L. Carmen Forcier~
(Copyright 1970)

THREE MONTHS ELAPSED…

Those who bring sunshine to the lives of others
cannot keep it from themselves.

~Devotional book for Women~

Three months elapsed since John and I broke up with each other; time passed, and there was no word from him, or through any of my friends.

Susan, my best friend at the time, lived across the street. One afternoon I went over to see her and her brother, Todd. When I explained how John had not yet contacted me, Todd took it upon himself to call John on the phone, reassuring me that he and John were good friends, and that he would sort this all out.

I stood by the phone while they conversed, which then turned into questioning John about he and I getting back together. When Todd finally hung up, I was so intense on finding out what John had said to him that in sheer desperation I asked, "What did he say? What did he say?"

Todd paused for a moment, and said, "John has just told me that he's ALREADY TOLD YOU that you two were breaking up for good!"

SO NOT TRUE!

Heart-broken as I was, I went back home, sat in the basement and cried for more than an hour. My mind could not wrap itself around this lie. So devastated was I, knowing I'd been cheated.

From the day John suggested we break up, I simply no longer wanted to live! My friends all knew my parents did not accept him and knew how weird they were. One of the last times I saw my friends (of course I had to be home at four pm on a Sunday), they'd said things like, "Tell your dad to make sure he locks up that toilet paper—and make sure you find the fuse to run the dryer. Oh! And do not kiss anyone—we would not want you to go to hell!" and more!

No one offered to walk me home. I felt very much alone and extremely sad! I'd lost my friends because my parents were SO CRUEL!

The glory of friendship is not the outstretched hand,
nor the kindly smile, nor the joy of companionship.
It is the spiritual inspiration that comes to one,
when one discovers that someone else believes in him/her
and is willing to trust him/her.

~Ralph Waldo Emerson~

A FEW WEEKS LATER…

To forgive is to set a prisoner free
And discover the prisoner was you.

~Devotional book for women~

A few weeks later, Todd asked me to go to a basketball game as a sort of kind of date. He'd always liked me, but I accepted his invitation as a friend only. When we arrived in the gym of Riverside High, Todd saw John in the seats, and walked up to him to say hello. But guess what? There was John sitting with a blonde girl, hand in hand! Immediately, I broke out in tears, and walked away, finding seats away from the two lovers. Was I ever upset!

On our way back home Todd said he would not take me out again because he saw that I was still in love with John! NO KIDDING, EH?

Through the grapevine, I heard that John's new girlfriend lived down my street, just one block away from my home. Also, there were rumours that he was sleeping with her as her parents were often away! The shock I felt I cannot describe. He had duped and dumped me, and yet I still loved him with all my heart!

I learned of his break-up with this girl about a year later. During the summer of 1970, one of my friends, Carole, who happened to live across the street from John's old girl-friend, saw John walking in the area. He met up with her and asked, "How is Carmen doing?" This memory still sustains me to this day, as his curiosity meant so much to my broken soul. Deep in my heart, I knew he still loved me and was sorry for having hurt us both so profoundly.

At times, while riding my friend's bike, I'd stop to say hello to John's kind mother, always looking for an opportunity to see John. On a few occasions, he stood in his backyard with his black dog although he never did turn to face me—nor could he even bring himself to say "Hi"—and he never acknowledged my presence. In the end, he may have suffered more than I. Who knows?

Because of the fondness we shared in our past relationship, I forgave him on all counts. Over all of these years, I've kept good memories of the two of us together, one of them being when he'd told me I was a fun-loving girl. He always remained deep in my heart—for how could I ever forget the true love we had for each other?

Decades later, even though I still have not found how to contact him, I am hopeful that one day this poem reaches his heart!

M. L. CARMEN FORCIER

FIRST TENDER LOVE

We met one summer's afternoon
In 1968
Your humour felt so warm to me
Your smile your wink your gaze.

Some time went by and then there was
A dance for all our friends
I stood not far from where you were
Loving your English accent

You then took time to look my way
My heart so very nervous
Guiding me to the dance floor
You were so very courteous.

Our first slow dance was "Hey Jude"
It played on and on
Feeling you so close to me
Created a strong bond

We'd walk together on winter's evenings
In wind and cold and snow
Always with arms around each other
So in love, you know.

Many times we'd walk and walk
Just to be together

The wind would blow, the snow would fall,
My head upon your shoulder

You made me feel so warm inside
My heart was so on fire
How I wanted to share with you,
All my heart's desires

You know how frightened I was then
Caught in doubt and terror
I never meant to hurt you so
Forgive me for my errors.

You were the most precious guy
I had ever met
I loved you more than anyone else
Oh how my heart regrets!

And then one day you stood so firm
And said we'd have to part
Only for three months, you said
And then again we'd start.

My heart so torn, so full of pain
I held my head up high
For I believed your word was true
That time would fast go by.

As I looked back to wave good-bye
You turned as well to see
Held back my tears for knew you well
So synchronized were we.

More than three months did go by
I could not wait much longer
A friend of ours reassured me then
He called you as a favour.

M. L. CARMEN FORCIER

As he hung up and looked at me
I asked, "What did he say?"
And Todd could hardly say the words,
To my greatest dismay

My mind confused, my heart so crushed
This was not the truth
You'd said to him that you'd told me
We were forever through.

I kept on loving you the same
Even though betrayed
Knowing that my parents were,
Causing of all this pain

About six months forward in time
I'd broken my left ankle
Was in a cast from hip to toe
Quite something to handle

As I was at Hotel Dieu
Grey shadows of a figure
Noticed near my door so close
It was your dearest mother.

She came to see me every day
By taking all her breaks
To visit with me...talk and stay
She was my saving grace.

Bless her heart for loving me
Through this kind of gesture
Always sitting close to me
This I will remember.

By now September has come and gone
I wore the cast three months
February 20, 1970
I'd met my future husband.

I was only fifteen then
And he was twenty-four
Had to finish all my studies
Grow up a little more.

Left home in '71,
Was almost seventeen
Went to live on the poorest side
With people who were mean.

School grades—no more honours
Although I did succeed
In obtaining enough credits,
To be accepted into nursing.

In March of '73 at last
Became a full-fledged nurse
And then the following month of June
Marriage then came first.

First child was born in January
1974
Three pounds she weighed and was so healthy;
We could not ask for more.

Two years later-November '75
Gave birth to second child
Another beautiful baby girl
This one twice the size (seven pounds)

There had been complications.
Was not to have another
But nature having its own mind
We surely did discover.

To the city of Ottawa
We moved from Toronto's suburbs
Found ourselves in Québec city
This was with greatest wonder.

M. L. CARMEN FORCIER

Québec city was our home
We loved it there so much
Third child was our first son
We were profoundly touched.

Then came an opportunity
To come out west to find
The weather here was so much better
We then found peace of mind.

Being so far from family
We saved our kids from shame
Saved our sanity and more
Our home here we did claim.

By this time–October '79
Six months then went by
And in April 1980
I was hospitalized.

The doctors didn't know the problem
Diagnosis unclear
My mind not well, was very ill,
Consumed with so much fear

In hospital I did remain
For a full six months
My children hardly knew me now
Sickness was a constant

Medication—I took tons
Yet was always suicidal
Then April 29,' 81
I OD'd to make it final.

Was saved by firemen who pumped
My stomach of the pills
Only five minute's time was left,
Before becoming still

New doctors analyzed my history
Consulted one another
Found that I'd been born with genes,
Causing the illness of Bipolar

Started taking proper meds
To help the swinging moods
Had always been with the same doctor
Who knew me through and through

Had worked in many hospitals
Toronto, Ottawa
Then found my place with newborn babies
And this was very special

In '84 a minor hit
From a passing car
Left my back in greatest pains,
My job, could not do anymore

In '85 and '86
Became "high" again
Two full years had to pass,
To clear things in my brain

My family was growing fast
My husband a great support
Throughout all my ups and downs
Always lived in comfort

Very few people like my self
Are loved as much as I
Most of them are left alone,
When challenges arise

My children, early on they learned
The symptoms, moods, behaviours
They'd guide me through when they could
They were my little saviours.

Was sick again in '96
Switched to a new med
It took me one full year and some
To stabilize again

My girls are now twenty-seven and twenty-five
My son, he's twenty-one
Forty years of married life
In June 2001

To add on here one small note
To say I'm now grandmother
September 4, '99
Boy—from second daughter

You're in my thoughts more often now
I even dream of you
And wonder how things might have been,
If again you were to choose

A few regrets-and lots of sorrow
At having lost you then
First love, we always carry forward
For it reminds us when

Life was free, young and easy
And hearts loved tenderly
Such big dreams and aspirations
Desired oh so dearly!

My deep felt gratitude to you
For the gentleman you were
Your kindness love and understanding,
Will be cherished forever

Here's trusting that you've been blessed
Many times over
And found the very peace of mind
We all want to discover.

Believe that your birthday is
This upcoming July
And that you will be celebrating,
Your fiftieth, dear child

Our inner selves remain the same
No matter what our age
I'm sure you're still a happy man,
Of wisdom and of grace

Today's the eighth of Jan '01
I'm researching to find
Where I can send word to you
I hope you do not mind.

Thanks again for *you* my friend
To whom I still feel so close
You've given me respect and love
For this I say, "Thank you."

My heart also wants to say
How much I loved you then
How much I love you still today
This love will never end.

The warmth of this first love for me
My heart feels every day
We met one summer's afternoon
In 1968

PS

Also when I think of you,
I see you as a Prof.
A history teacher was your dream
Did you ever pull it off?
Written for John Lianzi
my first boyfriend.

~ M.L. Carmen Forcier~
(Copyright January 8, 2001)

AS TEENAGERS...

*The greatest good we can do for others is
not to share our riches, but to assist in revealing their own.*

~Benjamin Disraeli~

BRACE YOURSELF!

As teenagers, my sister and I would take a shower every single day, as we always felt dirty and in need of a good washing. In our early twenties we were talking about this, and both of us were shocked to hear the other say that when we used to shower, we had never washed our pubic area! OH! My God! This is because, as children, we were always given baths; never once do we remember our parents washing this area of our bodies! We'd always been under the impression that it was a GREAT SIN to even think about this as part of our anatomy, let alone touch and wash it!

Now that's what I call CA-RAZY! GEEZ LOUISE!

★ ★ ★

When my sister and I were between the ages of ten and twelve, and up until we were fourteen and sixteen, we'd often come home to find unwrapped newspaper on the bathroom floor with a used sanitary napkin. My mom would yell at us for not using them to their full capacity.

She insisted we put them back on for our next menstrual cycles. This was too sick to even think of. We NEVER did re-use those pads!

ONE DAY...MY DAD...

*Our greatest glory is not in never failing
but in rising every time we fail.*

~Ralph Waldo Emerson~

One day, my dad had to get all of his teeth pulled, as he had not seen a doctor since forever and his mouth was a freaking mess. My mom decided to go out that evening and asked me to stay home and watch over my dad in case his gums started to bleed! This was a real punishment!

While speaking to one of my friends on the phone, explaining my circumstances, my dad had gotten up in the meantime and handed me a written note saying, "You do not have to stay home for me." I chose to stay home anyway, just in case.

A week or so later, my dad went back to work. That first day, after he came back home with his black lunch box, my mom asked me to clean it out. This was strange, as she ALWAYS did this herself. There I was, with my hands in his lunch box.

Lo and behold, I pick up a small jar filled with pinkish mucous, gobs and lumps! UGH! HOW SICKENING! It was so disgusting! Not knowing what it was, I threw it in the garbage. My mom saw me and yelled, saying that I had to empty the jar of its contents first so that I could wash it afterwards, because you see, she wanted me to be forever reminded that you do not throw anything away because, during the depression...etc.

I began explaining to her that we had many of these jars in the basement; why could my father not have spit this out at work, instead of taking it home? She remained furious with me, insisting that I had no idea what it meant to have less than nothing.

Even though she was right, her sadistic ways drove me crazy, asking me to clean this stuff up. I refused to do so, went downstairs, telling her she could clean my dad's "shit" herself and continue saving her pennies in her own sick way!

My sister and I had heard so much about the 1929 depression. They had stories of always saving money, always purchasing the ugliest painting because it was cheaper than the nice painting, or buying an ugly used teeny sofa for our visitors instead of something nice and wide enough to sleep comfortably.

★ ★ ★

Growing up, the depression was all we seemed to hear about; we were always told how spoiled we were and how we had everything, and did not know the value of a dollar…on and on without fail. They never grew out of it, never moved forward, and were glued to the past, with their minds stuck in a time warp!

As we grew older, we noticed other people their age who'd gone through these same difficult times; they were not negative about it but rather were thankful for what they DID have in the now.

My dad often mentioned that he could not stand eating spaghetti because his family ate so much of it during those tough years. Decades later, I truly realized that we had lived like kings while I was growing up.

We never lacked anything, and so my gratitude for all of my blessings began to emerge.

M. L. CARMEN FORCIER

DURING MY EARLY FORTIES...

If you can't feed a hundred people, then just feed one.

~Devotional book for women~

As we have therefore opportunity, let us do good unto all men.

~Galatians 6:10~

During my early forties, my mom shared with me one of her stories in regards to the economic depression of 1929. She stated in a very remorseful tone that as a small child of about ten, (born in 1921), she would leave the school grounds during lunch period and hide beneath the steps of her church so that no one could see her eating sandwiches made with heavy grease. This shamed her to no end!

★ ★ ★

Throughout the years my dad would talk about his mom who had died due to a malfunctioning valve in her heart. He was always close to tears when he spoke of her, having always regretted that she had not lived long enough to see my sister, though she'd seen me at the tender age of one. Another story of my dad's was when he talked about a baby sister he'd had who'd died of diarrhea at the age of eight months! This always made me very sad!

As mentioned earlier, my mother never had a kind word to say about anyone. There was always something wrong with other people. So critical was she that it affected my life in more ways than I could ever have imagined!

GOING BACK IN TIME...

Jesus can turn water into wine,
but he can't turn your whining into anything.

~Devotional book for Women~

When I was four years old, my Aunt Emma, who was married to my mom's brother, Eugene, was renting the top floor of my grandparent's house; she came downstairs to ask me if I wanted to go sliding on the ice with her and my cousin Paul. In my mind, I kept saying, *no, no, no,* because my mom could not stand the way this aunt of mine always spoke so loud and never seemed to let other people talk!

So, I'd learned to dislike her quite a bit. My response to her was that I did not have any boots to go out in the cold. Then, my grandmother sat me on her bed and pulled up a big box of shoes and boots she'd collected over the years. Only one pair fit me and they were bright red. So I said to my mémé, "I do not like the colour, therefore I'm not going to wear them." The true reason for my stubbornness was because my mom had me hating everyone

* * *

At the age of fourteen, my aunt Lilianne told me that from birth to the time I was five years of age (until I started school), my maternal grand-parents always came to pick me up to stay with them for long periods of time due to my father's heated temper and violent verbal abuse towards me. He especially could absolutely not tolerate the crying of a baby or small child, to the point where my mother had attached a soother around my neck till I was four. As soon as I felt the need to cry, I would plug my mouth with my own hands, arresting my inner sobs, always in great fear that my father would yell at me!

I'd promised my aunt Lilianne to never tell my dad the secret of my living with my grand-parents!

When living with my mémé and pépé most of the time as a toddler, it may not have been only because of my father's temper but also due to my mother's swinging moods, THEN and NOW!

★ ★ ★

In the fall of 1965, when I was aged fifteen, my father had just blamed me for something I had not done. I was so angry, I broke my promise to my aunt regarding my mémé and pépé, when still a small child. Immediately, my dad ordered me to kneel on the basement cemented floor, yelled, screamed, and hollered for at least half an hour trying to convince me how much both my parents loved me, as he showed me where he'd written my first words. Years later, one of my doctors told me to never humiliate myself in such a way, ever again!

Do you see how destructive a negative attitude towards life becomes when you teach a child to dislike or hate someone? I carried these feelings on for years until one day, while on holiday for five weeks at my aunt Lilianne and uncle John place (as they were then living in Chicoutimi P. Québec), I was criticizing people left and right, sounding like an absolute b★★★★.

My aunt Liliane immediately picked up on this and asked me a few questions re: two of my aunts. In regards to my aunt Emma, my aunt Lilianne said, "Do you realize that your uncle always had a weak heart due to having had Rheumatic Fever as a child? He could not keep a job for very long..." and she continued by saying how my aunt always took care of him in their home, while raising four children; how was she still able to keep her house clean?

Then I mentioned how my aunt Peggy never spoke a word of French and how this irritated my mother so very much. My aunt Lilianne then asked me if my aunt Peggy would ever ask me how I was doing in school; my response was that she was always interested in what my sister and I did. These few positive thoughts had an enormous impact on the rest of my life, because from then on, I would always look for the good in people, having been so shocked to learn anyone had any good habits!

PEACEFUL
PONDERING
PAUSE

To love one's self is the beginning is the beginning of a lifelong romance.

~Oscar Wilde~

Excerpt from book, entitled:
GIFT FROM THE SEA

Written by
~ANNE MORROW LINDBERGH~

Copyright 1955/1975; copyright renewed 1983.

The following are written in the author's very own words,
Copied from pages,--50-51

"If one sets aside time for a business appointment, a trip to the hairdresser, a social engagement, or a shopping expedition, that time is accepted as inviolable. But if one says: I cannot come because that is my hour to be alone one is considered rude, egotistical or strange. What a commentary on our civilization, when being alone is considered suspect; when one has to apologize for it, make excuses, hide the fact that one practices it--like a secret vice. Actually, these are among the most important times in one's life when one is alone. Certain springs are tapped only when we are alone. The artist knows he must be alone to create; the writer, to work out his thoughts; the musician, to compose; the saint, to pray. But women need solitude in order to find again the true essence of themselves...

End of excerpt.

* * *

A wise man will hear,
and will increase learning;
and a man of understanding,
shall attain unto wise counsels.

~Proverbs 1:5~

* * *

When you find the way
Others will find you.
Passing by on the road
They will be drawn to your door.
The way that cannot be heard
Will be echoed in your voice
The way that cannot be seen
Will be reflected in your eyes

~Lao-Tzu~

* * *

Taken from book entitled
Real Magic
Written by ~Dr. Wayne W. Dyer~

From pages

184 & 186

HOW CHILDREN FAIL

We destroy the love of learning in children, which is so strong when they are small, by encouraging and compelling them to work for petty and contemptible rewards—gold stars, or papers marked

100 and tacked to the wall, As on report cards, or honour rolls, or deans lists--- in short, for the ignoble satisfaction of feeling that they are better than someone else.

Written by
~Dr. Wayne W. Dyer~

"There it is that business of getting people to believe that they are better than others. You very likely have bought into this big lie in some areas of your life. How could you deserve to think of yourself as a special divine necessity when you didn't measure up to the way others were performing or looking? You learned to compare yourself with others and even to believe that this is only human nature. It is the very thing that has not allowed you to develop a self-concept based upon being valuable, deserving and divine"

Written by ~John Holt~
Brief notation…

At an early age, my music teacher had entered me in a small piano recital! As I sat on the piano bench on stage, my fingers got too nervous and I came in fourteenth. The awful disappointed and shameful look on my mom's face horrified me!

From page 204

Applying Prosperity Principles in your daily life…
~Paramhansa Yogananda~ put it in these words:

"Possession of material riches, without inner peace, is like dying of thirst while bathing in a lake. If material poverty is to be avoided, spiritual poverty is to be abhorred! For, it is spiritual poverty not material lack that lies at the core of all human suffering."

MEMORIES
IN
MOTION

COMING BACK TO THE FACT...

*The will of the Source never takes you
where the grace of the Source will not protect you.*

~Anonymous~

I used to pull out all of my lashes, and I would also do other things that made me feel pain, such as numbing one of my legs to sleep in order to feel the pins and needles, which prevented me from walking properly. I would also do this on the school bus going back home; when the bus driver helped me cross the busy street, I could barely walk, my leg was so numb. I literally limped my way towards the other side. I was always terrified of getting hit by a car!

On other occasions I would bite into my cheeks, and hold tight with my teeth until I bled. Today, I have four scars on both sides of my inner cheeks; two of them near the top, two more near the bottom.

OFTEN TIMES, I WOULD REMEMBER...

Feeling is the secret.

~Neville Goddard~

Oftentimes, I would remember some events from my early childhood; looking at my dad's face while describing my memories out loud, I would interpret his expression as a look of total fear, as if he wanted me to shut up; he may have thought I might remember things HE definitely did not want me to speak of!

I'm going to attempt to describe what I started feeling at the age of forty-five. I was seeing my psychiatrist one afternoon and I really wanted to talk about how I felt inside, regarding my father.

The words just came out:

"I think my father sexually abused me below the age of two!"

My doctor took one stunned look at me and responded by saying,

"Do not go there. Do not even *try* to dig up these memories."

Even so, I persisted in asking myself why these doubts were in my heart.

At the age of seven or eight, my sister and two of our friends played with a little girl called Mercedes. I'd never spoken of this story to anyone EVER! It felt really eerie discussing this in the open with my doctor.

I began by telling him that we would take little Mercedes down to our basement because we wanted her to love us SO VERY MUCH. We would sit her down in a small, dark, cold cellar, close the door, and listen to her crying until she would stop and fall asleep. Then we'd open the door (saving her, as we felt we were doing) telling her how much we were sorry and how we cared for her so very much, caressing her, saying she was a good girl and that we loved her. A few moments would pass and then we'd repeat the act over and over again for about an hour or more.

No one knew about this as my mother was always busy doing her hairdressing upstairs, and we certainly chose our time to make sure my dad was not arriving from work.

We would do this maybe once a week; we knew what we were doing to this small child was not right, although we got TONS of satisfaction in doing this to this little girl. It was as if I had a GREAT URGE to punish someone and then BE THEIR SAVIOUR, all loving and kind.

When my psychiatrist heard my story, he said,

"Whatever happens in a child's life, while growing up, she/he tends to imitate the same behaviour they've experienced with their parents as toddlers. Whatever actions were done to a small child at a very tender age, this child will tend to repeat on someone else, as he/she is growing up, because they FEEL very strongly and also NEED to retaliate against someone as emotionally vulnerable as they had been AND punish others for their inner frightened emotions."

I felt so guilty and ashamed while speaking these words because we'd instilled so much fear into this small child.

And so, here lies my hypothesis in regards to my dad, with the idea that he was having sexual desires for me as a small infant. First off, he would often, throughout my life, put his arm around my shoulders telling people how beautiful I had been as a toddler, especially when my mom did my hair up in ringlets!

Secondly, my parents often fought! My dad would constantly SCREAM WITH GREAT ANGER at my mom—especially Sunday mornings, repeating over and over, "You do not want to come back to me!" while my mother sat at the kitchen table crying out loud. These were the ONLY times I enjoyed taking care of my sister as these fights would scare the living daylights out of me! Even though I was about seven or eight when all of this was going on, I knew my mother did not want to have sex with my dad.

When I was between the ages of two and four years of age, when we were living in our first house, my father would often open up the kitchen floor to go down into a small dark cold cellar. I would often watch him turn the light on and then choose the canning goods my mom had made in the summertime. Most of the canned goods purchased at the store were also found here.

I always asked my dad if I could go down there with him. Every time I'd ask, his response was always a very clear "NO!" He said that it was too cold for me, and he asked if I could just stop asking him the same question every time he went down there!

So here's my theory:

My dad had once told me he'd discovered liquor in the army, and how he absolutely loved the way it made him feel, forgetting all the pains of being a soldier at war. Two of my dad's brothers were alcoholics, and my father had once said to my sister that his own dad used to walk around the house with a bottle in hand.

Now, here's another part of this nightmare! I explained to my doctor that the smell of certain liquor on the breath of other people really excited me sexually; additionally, the first time I saw an alcoholic person on TV, when I was at the age of thirteen or so, I felt very sensuous and actually had my first orgasm. I had no idea what was happening to me! OK, now you have to remember this next part. There are certain smells of liquor on people's breath which, to this day, do not feel threatening to me although I'm ALWAYS TERRIFIED if ever a drunk passes close to me—no matter what kind of alcohol they have been drinking

Certain liquor odours absolutely scared me to death while others caused me to have orgasms. Now, mixed in with all of this was my mom who said that sex was a sin, hated being touched in any way shape or form, rejected my father's sexual approaches time and time again AND never discussed the birds and the bees with neither myself nor my sister, as this was a sinful subject to talk about!

Going back to the small, cold and dark cellar, although I do not remember being sexually abused, the fact remains that certain liquor smells make me have orgasms. This is very puzzling to me and also to my doctor. My theory is that my father would bring me down into the small cold, dark cellar in our first home, after having a few swigs of alcohol, AND would possibly then touch me in the sexual areas of my body.

When I got married, I was ALSO uncomfortable with my husband (sexually). This feeling went on for about eight years. Luckily for me, he was not a drinker!

You have to remember that, according to my mother, French kissing, having sex, dancing close to a boy's body, etc. guaranteed an eternity in hell!

M. L. CARMEN FORCIER

*An architect knows that if he builds with care,
his structure may stand for centuries. A teacher knows
that if he builds with love and truth,
what he builds will last forever.*

~John W. Shlatter~

WHILE THREE OF MY GIRLFRIENDS...

*Be kind to yourself. Look in the mirror
and see that you are beautiful...*

~Linda Ann McConnell~

While three of my girlfriends from school were visiting me in hospital, I told them that my very hunky doctor would be in soon. As I spoke, there he was; my friends immediately stopped talking, and their mouths dropped by two inches—I swear!

They were dumfounded to see how good-looking he really was! I was so proud! He had asked me if he could be the first to sign my cast. As I'd shared some of my poetry with him over time, his signature on the cast said, *To the Poetess.*

One evening he came to sit with me for a couple of hours, just talking about things in general. This was unusual for a doctor to sit with a patient as if he were a visitor! He mentioned that he loved my poetry; I said that I'd just discovered that the inside of a hospital was like a world unto its own. He liked that analogy.

We got along very well, although you have to remember that I was not quite fifteen years of age, and he was about twenty-eight at the time. I had a huge crush on him right up until I left Windsor for a higher education.

As I was leaving his office for the last time, I mentioned I would not be back. His shocked response was, "Never?"

I said "Yes," and then thanked him from the bottom of my heart for all the years he'd cared for me as a patient.

PART TWO

REVERSE AND GO AGAIN...

The things we overcome in life become our strengths.

~Anne Bancroft~

Before I said good-bye to my GP, so much had happened!

It was the summer of 1970. I was nearing my seventeenth birthday. One day, all four of us in the family had it out, and it was not a pretty picture. My sister started to struggle with my mom's arms and I was doing the same with my father.

Eventually my sister cried out to my dad, "Leave her alone!" At the same time, she aimed for my dad's crotch and kicked him real hard. She missed it by a few inches.

Finally, I ran to my bedroom, while my sister hurried down to our haven, the basement; pulling my jeans up, I raced out of the house before my dad could stop me. I ran as fast as I could to my friend Susan's house directly across the street. I was crying so hard and just could not stop.

Susan's mother was there when I arrived, and once I'd calmed down, she said these words to me: "One day, this will all make you a better person." This was a sentence I could not comprehend at all!

Later on that evening, I went home, as it was nearly 10 pm. While approaching the back door, there stood my dad with a big, long piece of wood in his hands. He was propping it up while giving me a dirty angry look, making it impossible for me to enter.

I ran back to Susan's asking if I could stay the night, explaining what had just happened. Her whole family juggled the room spaces around on the main floor and in the basement so that Susan and I could sleep in the same bed.

IT HAD GOTTEN TO
THE POINT...

Nothing happens unless first a dream.

~Carl Sandberg~

It had gotten to the point where I found it hard to breathe, being surrounded by my parents who were always so angry at both my sister and I. A few months earlier, my dad had said to me, "If you do not want to follow the rules of this house then go live somewhere else!"

Taking this literally, almost like permission, I saw a chance to get out of this sick family situation. A few days later, I said to my dad that I wanted to go to my mémé's house; and so began my journey into the unknown world out there. I was packing my dad's big Chrysler trunk with all of my possessions for about ninety minutes while my dad sat at the wheel waiting for me to finish—AS IF he did not know my intentions!

Before leaving, my mom realized what I was doing, stopped me and said, "One of your daughters, later on, will leave you the same way you are leaving home now!"

This did not frighten me in the least. My determination was stronger than ever; I was as angry as anyone could be!

Upon arriving at my grand-mother's house, I started unloading my stuff— would you believe that my dad helped me settle into the room upstairs where I would live for a short while? Amazing, eh? Yep! He nonchalantly acted as if nothing, hypocrite that he was.

Settling into my new surroundings, I felt very proud of myself; finally I was out of that prison and free to be the good person I'd always been, barely ever having been treated decently.

This was the beginning of my way to lash back at my parents to the core of their being, embarrassing them in front of friends and family.

Soon, I became aware that if someone hurt me deeply, I could hurt them back even more!

My father came back three days later, asking my grand-mother to convince me to go back home. When she told me this, I was very emotional and said that I could not possibly go back! She said she understood, reminding me of the year when I was approximately eight, the day my father had caught my sister and I with two cousins of ours, walking around a block where there was traffic—which he'd specified earlier on not to do.

We had disobeyed his order, and thus my dad slapped me on my behind from the corner, all the way to my mémé's. Apparently one of my uncles was looking out the window, hearing me screaming and crying. His very words were, "One day, Roland (my father) will have great problems with Carmen."

Arriving at the house, no one said a peep! I ran to the washroom, locked the door and cried my heart out, as I was so humiliated in front of my mom's family!

IT HAD BEEN THREE WEEKS...

*Gratitude is a blessing
that nourishes the heart, mind, and soul.*

~M. L. Carmen Forcier~

It had been three weeks since I'd moved in with my grandparents. I was sleeping up in the attic, which had been re-done into one large room for guests needing a bed. I usually slept quite deeply!

One morning, after my mémé's many attempts at calling my name, I finally woke up with a start, and ran down the stairway so fast that when I got to the kitchen, I was out of breath.

My mémé was standing behind my pépé who was kneeling, head forward. As I asked him if he was alright, his head kept going back and forth, saying, "No, no, no!"

His right hand was holding his chest to the left. I had no idea what was going on; I looked at mémé for answers, though she just stood still, looking out a window, worried and alone, with her hand on one of my pépé's shoulders. From her expression, my mind started racing. I knew I had to call for help!

Running to the telephone, I was so nervous that the phone fell to the floor, and I thought I'd unplugged it! I looked up my aunt Peggy's phone number in my mémé's little black book, because this aunt was a former nurse.

When she answered the phone, I desperately said that pépé was in pain and could not talk. He then fell to the kitchen floor! My aunt said she would call an ambulance and asked me to get all of pépé's medications ready for the hospital doctors. As I hung up, I went to remove my pépé's eyeglasses, feeling very useless and frightened.

My mémé was still standing in the same spot, unable to speak; so there I was, just staring at both of them, frantically waiting for the ambulance attendants to arrive.

It seemed like twenty minutes before they finally got there, and when they did appear, they were having a really hard time lifting my pépé up onto the gurney, as he was very tall and heavy.

When my mémé showed me where pépé's pills were, I gathered them and handed the vials to the two medics. My mémé, who still had not said a word since I'd run downstairs, accompanied them in the ambulance.

As they were pulling out of the driveway, my aunt Peggy and uncle Léo were upon the scene. I jumped into their car and we sped away, red lights and all!

Four days went by before he passed away. The whole family was there. When our turn came, Richard and I, hand in hand, went to see our Pépé for the last time. I kissed him on the forehead and Richard laid his hand on Pépés chest. It was an awkward moment; we had been so close to him and loved his happiness towards life.

Upon leaving the hospital, my mémé asked if I would live with her from now on; one of my aunts was shaking her head, so I responded with a "no." Besides, I was determined to leave all of my family behind so as not to see nor talk with my parents whenever they would visit my mémé and pépé in the future!

{Looking back, I could have lived with my grand-mother...and go to my room in the attic upstairs whenever my family visited!}

NOT LONG AFTER THIS…

As long as friends are spending time together,
the world will always be a bright and shining place.

~Barbara J. Hall ~

Guess what? I told my best friend Susan, who lived across the street that I was going to go to Madeleine's to see if she could help me out. (Remember Madeleine? She was my mother and father's former friend.)

I had dinner with her that same evening; she explained that she'd broken up with her boyfriend eons ago, and had never married. She kept repeating that in the present moment, she'd have a daughter like myself had she said "yes" to the man who'd been courting her at the time. This break-up happened the day I was born!

She knew of a social worker, and referred me to her by making an appointment for me. A few days later, as I was still living with my mémé, I took the bus downtown, and explained my home situation to this social worker while the tears rolled down my face. This woman immediately arranged for my parents to come to her office to discuss my situation.

They did come, though only to give me heck for not having come to them in the first place—*before* I'd left for mémé's. There had never been a conversation in our family between both my sister and I and my parents, so it had never dawned on me to approach them, as they were mean, distant, and very negative towards life in general.

Catholic religion ruled big-time in our house; the message was "Shut-up and listen and do not talk back or you'll get a spanking, you little devils!" etc.

They left the office by saying "Merry Christmas" which hurt to the bone for them and for me; there was so much pain in all of us!!!

This social worker reminded me that one day I would need my parents, and she was right!

If you talk to the animals, they will talk to you,
and you will know each other. If you do not talk to them,
you will not know them, and what you do not know,
you will fear. What one fears one destroys.

~Chief Dan George ~

MY BEST FRIEND IN
HIGH SCHOOL...

When one is out of touch with oneself,
one cannot touch others.

~Ann Morrow Lindbergh~

My best friend in high school was Ginette. She'd convinced her own mom to take me in for my last year of school—grade twelve. One evening, a car pulled up at mémé's with Ginette, her mom, and dad.

Ginette helped carry all of my belongings down the stairs and into her car. This took a good hour, and then we were off to Ginette's home. I do not remember saying good-bye to my mémé! All I could think of was FREEDOM AT LAST!

Meanwhile, back at the ranch, and while sitting in Ginette's living room, I phoned my music teacher to let her know I was no longer going to take piano lessons. Then the school priest called me and asked if there was anything he could do to remedy the situation. My response was that it was too late.

Then my mom made an appointment for me to see the principal of my original high school whom I did see; I repeated the same words I'd used with the priest. Again my mom arranged for me to see another older priest who used to be in our parish, now working at the hospital where I was born. I went to see him also, but this time I was fed up with all of these

BEING BIPOLAR

people who suddenly seemed to care about my wellbeing! I lectured him in a very angry tone, saying that my situation had nothing to do with him, and to mind his own business! I felt so very satisfied that I'd put him in his place!

★ ★ ★

Now, it had been understood with Ginette's family that I was welcome to stay with them till I finished grade twelve at a new high school, because I was now living in a different neighbourhood. I was making $102 per month from welfare. Ginette's mom asked me for $20 per week to help pay for my food, etc. That left me with $22 per month, plus the baby bonus of $10 (which the government gave to each family with children for clothing and personal items).

The day of my birthday, Ginette's mom made a peanut-butter cake for me. A few days later, it was Ginette's birthday, and there was a big party with lots of family and friends. This was hard for me—plus afterwards, Ginette and her mom went for a walk together. I could feel they'd come to an agreement of some sort.

About two weeks later, Ginette's mom seated us differently for dinner. As we started to eat, her mom came straight out and said that it was understood from the beginning that I was to find a place to live (having lived with them for only a few months!).

I was so upset and frightened. I ran upstairs, locked myself in the bathroom, and started crying, crying, and crying, in total shock. I could not believe what had just been decided!

The mom then yelled at me to come back downstairs to finish my dinner, but I never did go back down until the next day, when Ginette, one of her sisters, and I walked to school as usual. My feelings were those of betrayal, loneliness, disappointment and anger! I was devastated, with absolutely nowhere to turn, and was definitely scared out of my wits!!

Ginette and I shared a bed, and it was a living hell in this household with all of this tension going on. She and her sisters would scream at me to go and get a place of my own, and to leave them alone and be on my way!

As luck would have it, one of Ginette's brothers, Robert, was married and lived close by. He and his wife Diane both came to take me looking for another place to stay. The only one we found was a boarding house full of marijuana smoke, with single beds in every room, and a shared kitchen and bathroom. The smoke alone had Robert saying I could not live there!

On the way home, Diane asked me if I'd like to stay with THEM, as they had an extra room in their apartment. At the same time, she let me know that it would cost me $25 per week instead of the $20 per week I was used to paying Ginette's family. This left me $2.00 plus the $10 baby bonus per month.

The following few days were very difficult, as Robert's mother TOTALLY did not approve of this arrangement. She wanted me in the streets, she was that angry.

On my last night there, I asked Ginette what had caused her mother to change her mind so suddenly. Her answer was that usually her dad was often angry, and that the moment I moved in, his anger dissipated and the whole family felt I was the reason he'd become very gentle! Go figure!

Personally, I thought they were all nuts!

The following quotes and passages were taken from the book called...

WISDOM of the AGES
Copyright (1998)

From page 94
What if you slept?
And what if,
In your sleep
You dreamed?
And what if, in your dream,
You went to heaven
And there plucked
A strange and
Beautiful flower
And what if,
When you awoke,
You had the flower
In your hand

—Samuel Taylor Colerridge
(1772–1834)

IF YOU DO NOT STAND FOR SOMETHING (SIGNIFICANT)
YOU MAY FALL FOR ANYTHING...
(UNWORTHY OF YOUR TRUE SELF)

Part author...

~M. L. Carmen Forcier~
(Copyright 2011)

PART THREE

ENCOUNTERS
of the
ESSENCE

NOW, YOU HAVE TO REMEMBER...

I hear and I forget. I see and I remember.
I do and I understand.

~Chinese proverb~

Now, you have to remember that John and I never got back together. This made me desperate to find another boyfriend so that I could again feel that love and closeness. I was now fifteen and a half years old; it was 1970.

One Saturday afternoon, in the basement of our little French church, there was a contest going on for who would be chosen to go to Toronto for two weekends in a row to meet up with other teens of our age to participate in discussions about the future life of our French language.

Those who were chosen for this special trip had to pick the highest card from a deck. I had picked the queen of clubs, and a girl beside me picked an ace; and so, at that moment she was one of the lucky people who would take these two trips! Darn it! I was SO SURE I'd WIN!

A few days later, I received a call from the director of this contest; he informed me that I'd been chosen to go to Toronto, as the girl who'd won was not allowed to take the trip due to her low grades.

So there it was: all I had to do now was convince my parents to let me go—not such a simple task as you well may know by now! The director, whose name was Lucien Gava, came to my home, and after two hours, convinced my father into letting me go on these two weekend trips.

We were three Francophone girls chosen from Windsor to attend these seminars. We took the train to Toronto and someone was supposed to meet three French-speaking girls at Toronto, Ontario's huge train station.

Walking toward the ramp to get our suitcases, I noticed a really good-looking guy walking not too far from us with his navy jacket over one of his shoulders.

In English, I said, "Look at that guy—he thinks he's king shit!"

As we got closer to the ramp, a young girl with two guys heard us speaking French, and approached us, asking if we were the girls from Windsor. As I extended my hand to the first guy, he just gave me the PEACE sign. I tried a second time to shake his hand and he repeated his gesture.

To myself, I said, *OH! My God!* This was the same guy I had just pointed out to the other two girls, saying how he thought he was the king of the world!

The other guy, Gérard, finally saved the day, took my hand, and we all acquainted ourselves quickly, as the guy with the navy jacket (named Alan) had to go to the airport after dropping us off at the seminary where we were to stay for the following two weekends.

The first time I looked into his eyes between his PEACE signs, and within those few seconds, I knew we would one day marry. He was twenty-four and I was only fifteen. No matter, I was determined and felt a HUGE desire to be with him.

As we were walking up the ramp, one of the two other girls who'd traveled with me said very forcefully, "You take your eyes off Alan 'cause I want him all to myself."

HA! In my mind, I thought, *You are not going to command me this way, because I have absolutely fallen head over heels for this guy; he's mine, and I WILL marry him!*

The date we met was February 20, 1970.

On the first weekend, Alan had to go to a northern city in Ontario, called Penetanguisheen, to meet with another group of teenagers. As I saw him walk out the door, going down a long hallway—again, with his navy coat over his shoulder, seeming happy as a lark—I thought to myself, *Will I ever see him again?*

Well, the following weekend, who do you think shows up playing pool in the lounge? Alan! I asked him if he was here for the full second weekend, and he said, "Yes."

OH! MY GOD! My dream had come true!

I had brought some of my music books with me. He came close to the piano and mentioned that he loved the classics. Of course, I preferred the Beatles.

Over the weekend we were in small groups, discussing many things; among them was how to animate a group of people when they start getting bored. As the meeting was almost at an end, Alan walked in to see how things were going with the couple he'd found in Montréal to give us these educational courses.

When class was dismissed, I walked up to Alan and asked him to sign my autograph book. This is what he wrote:

Avant d'aimer l'amour
Il faut aimer l'amitié
J'aime l'amitié
Donc je t'aime bien.

TRANSLATION

Before loving love
You must first love friendship
I love friendship
Therefore I love you.

These words confirmed his feelings towards me and reinforced my burning desire to live with this young man for the rest of my life!

We all attended an evening of dancing and fun, although something happened on the way there. See, we were all staying at a seminary for those two weekends, and one of the young priests came along with us. En route to the dancing hall, this priest had his arm around my shoulders all along, whispering to me in my ear that he wanted thirteen children with ME!

OK! So now, I was freaked out and too embarrassed to dance with him AND he would not take no for an answer! Finally, I stood up and turned the large table, where we were sitting with others, completely over on its side, making a big bang! Here's a possible example of someone who is Bipolar, who *may* react to this kind of situation in such a drastic, angry and intense way.

I ran to the washroom crying. The same girl, Lise, who'd warned me about not approaching Alan, followed me.

This is when I told her what the priest had insisted on saying to me and how pushy he was! She finally said that Alan was willing to take me for a cup of coffee, since I was so upset!

Now, you have to remember that this girl Lise liked to flirt with Alan, as he was the biggest hunk there, and she was quite pretty herself.

So off we went, Alan and I. He bought me a plate of fries, which I drowned with ketchup. He asked me what kind of music I preferred, and of course I said, "Rock and Roll." He then said that he preferred Beethoven, Mozart, Chopin, etc.

As the weekend came to a close, Alan drove the couple of instructors he had hired from Montréal to the Toronto airport. As we waited to be taken to the train station, there was another young man called Clément Trudeau who really fancied me, but I was dramatically in love with Alan. My heart was set and my mind determined!

Clément had the ability to make me laugh and laugh until it hurt, which is why he thought I could be his girl-friend!

The following year, another gathering was scheduled to occur in Toronto, though this time at York University. Again, I was chosen to represent Windsor, Ontario, by friends of our French church.

SO, THERE WE WERE...

Careful what you set your heart upon,
for it surely shall be yours.

~Ralph Waldo Emerson~

So, there we were, the same three girls on our way to Toronto via train, once again, only this time we were going to go to York University for our French Canadian gathering. The date was June 1971.

On the way there, Lise says to me, "Alan will be there." My response was, "You already have a boyfriend!" She answered by saying, "That does not matter!" If she only knew how determined I was to be Alan's wife someday. Growing up, my mother had repeatedly said to me, "You always get your way," which in fact was and still is true today!

Upon arriving, Lucien introduced me to a guy named Jean-François. Oh my God! He was so good-looking and looked like a real gentleman, highly-recommended, and all! I kind of fell for him as well, although my first choice was always Alan.

On that particular Saturday, Alan had spent the day filming the surrounding areas, and when evening came, we all sat to watch his "chef d'oeuvre"—and guess what? Alan came to sit between Jean-François and myself. All of a sudden, Alan had his arm around me and kissed me quite nicely. At that moment, Jean-François got up and walked away. I presumed he was vexed I'd chosen Alan over him.

During the last debate, which took place on the Sunday afternoon, we were placed in groups of four to five people. A girl by the name of Alice had a terrible crush on Alan (as did so many others) She was sitting next to where Alan was although she relented the space to me so that I could be in Alan and Jean-François's group.

He and I kept staring at each other, and Alan would spend his time putting my head down so as to prevent me from communicating any feelings towards Jean-François. We simply kept looking at each other all the same.

This went on for almost two hours. It was kind of nice to see that two guys were interested in me and my self in them both!

When it was time to say our goodbyes, Jean-François kissed me on the lips very hard. He had accepted his defeat, letting me know he would have loved me had I chosen him. As I approached Alan, I cried uncontrollably and would not let him go. Jean-François saw the whole scene.

I thought I would never see Alan again; he lived in Toronto and I in Windsor. I was so disheartened that it felt like the end of my life!

As our car drove away, I looked back; there was Alan waving. Did he want me or did he not? I would not know, for sure, for another full year!

EVERY DAY, I WOULD SPRINT HOME...

Forgiveness is the fragrance the blossom leaves on the sole,
after it has crushed the flower.

~Margaret Fishback Powers~

Every day, I would sprint home from the bus stop to see if Alan had written to me; every single day for a year I thought only of him. Talk about a burning desire! He was in my mind and heart for that whole year!

Then we had a conference in my hometown of Windsor, and so Alan came from Toronto to participate as a guide. It was fall of 1971. I was beside myself. There I was at the age of sixteen and a half, seeing the one I loved once again.

A couple for whom I often baby-sat had a room available for Alan to rent. The meetings were always interesting, and when the weekend came to a close, Alan borrowed Lucien's car, which permitted us go to my parents' house for him to meet my mom and dad.

At that time, my mom was very depressed (as I'd just left home that summer). She was still in shock about that whole horrible situation. She reminded Alan of a neighbour he'd had as a child who'd been in and out of psychiatric hospitals, who one day shot herself in the head with the family's rifle, back when Alan was about ten years old.

While we walked back to the car, I said to Alan that he should open the car door for me as my parents were both standing at the door looking in our direction.

Now it was June of 1972. I was seventeen and a half years old. I'd been living with Diane and Robert for nine months. They had so many rules I had to follow! First of all, my lunches for school were forever and always two sandwiches with meat spread on them.

Because I was still attending the same school as Ginette and her sisters, they certainly did not help the situation. One day, one of the sisters screamed out at me in the hallway and said the word "B****" really loud so that most of the students who were between classes could hear her speak so vehemently, loud and clear!

When I got home at Robert and Diane's, I told them what had happened at school. Robert immediately went to his mom's place, giving hell to the three sisters, insisting forcefully to leave me alone!

As for lunch hour, I'd gone to the cafeteria the first day I was on my own. I knew no one in particular and felt so out of place, and spotted Ginette and her sisters eating with their friends; due to this situation, I chose to eat my dry sandwiches in one of my classrooms upstairs.

Approximately one month later, the strict German principal, whom everyone feared, walked in on me while I was eating. His words were the following: "Students are not allowed to eat in classrooms as there have been many reports of students stealing items from teachers' desks!"

My response was, "Are you accusing me of stealing?" He responded with some shock to my question and said no, I was not a suspect. Even so, I kept going to this classroom every day from mid-October 1972, to the beginning of June 1973. When classes closed for the summer, I had made it through and felt GREAT relief

Just before the end of the last semester, we were asked by our teacher to present a speech of about six minutes in front of the class. As I'd been corresponding with Diane's brother (who at the time was incarcerated), I chose to write a speech on life as an inmate.

I practiced it so often, as it had to be delivered without any notes. This was to be the first important speech of my life. I knew no one in this class, which made me very nervous.

As I began speaking, I walked down every aisle, starting on my left, looking into every single student's eyes; then I walked toward the front on another aisle and so on until the whole class had seen my eyes meeting theirs row upon row.

I had practiced to finish exactly at the moment I was back in front of the classroom. And OH! My God! I could not believe my eyes and ears. EVERONE was standing, clapping, whistling, cheering and the teacher at the back of the classroom was so stunned...he'd never seen anything like it in all his years as a professor! He walked up to me, still clapping with the rest of the class, and shook my hand while asking me, "How in the world did you ever come up with such an idea?"

I smiled at him and said, "I do not know!"

The class kept cheering and whistling for at least three or four minutes minimum. I was very proud of myself as the whole point to my speech was to reach every student's heart. I felt accepted for the first time in this school where I'd felt so strange with its advanced political and historical classes.

In those moments, I received the most recognition I'd ever had. It was WONDERFUL. I'd reached every single student and they were so shocked by my presentation, unable to get over it! As friendless as I was, now at least this class knew what I was made of!

VISIONARY VOCATION

THE LAST THREE MONTHS...

*The flower of light in the field of darkness
has given me the strength to carry on.*

~Johnny Cash~ (while in prison)

In the last three months of the school year, I'd applied to take a Registered Nursing Assistant course, as it is called in Ontario. In Detroit, and in other provinces of Canada, they go under the name of LPN, which stands for Licensed Practical Nurse. I'd sent two application forms—one to London, Ontario, Canada, and the other to Scarborough General Hospital, as my dreamboat, Alan, lived in Scarborough, which is a suburb of Toronto, Ontario, Canada.

Eventually I was accepted by both schools, about one month before my high school years came to an end. Of course, I chose Scarborough General, as this would bring me closer to the one I loved.

Then, an interesting thing happened. When I got home from school on those last few days, there was an envelope for me from Scarborough General saying that they'd set up an interview to meet with me on a particular day—which was that very day. It only dawns on me now that Diane must have withheld from me this important mail, as she did not particularly like me, although the $100 I gave her and Robert every month was a GRAND GIFT for them!

I called the nursing school and explained my situation; they re-booked me for another appointment due three weeks later.

A few months before this occurred, Robert and Diane had decided that I was to have only one glass of milk a day, with no second helpings, AND now I was forced to wash my long hair in the bathtub instead of the kitchen sink. Even though I explained to them that this was very painful for me, it did not matter one single bit! Years later, I'd discover that I have mild scoliosis in my upper back—thus the severe pain!

NOW...THINGS GET REAL SPOOKY...

I shall pass through this world but once;
Any good therefore that I can do, let me do it now..
for I shall not pass this way again.

~Unknown~

One evening, my dad called me on the phone saying that a young woman had called my mom that day to say that I was pregnant! Who was this mysterious person?

My dad had to leave work and get medication for my mom to help her calm down. After denying these allegations, my dad came to pick me up and took me for some fish and chips. We had a nice conversation. He then drove me back to Robert's.

Before saying my final goodbyes to Robert and his wife, they'd just purchased a motorcycle and an air conditioning machine! Take a wild guess. Yep—they'd probably saved all of my rent money, because during all the time I lived with them, Robert was going to night school!

★ ★ ★

And so life went on. I finally took the Greyhound bus to Toronto, where Alan met me with his friend's car and drove me to my future nursing school for the important interview. After three hours of tests, questions, and inquiries, I was accepted into the Scarborough General nursing program!

THE DAY I LEFT WINDSOR…

Integrity of the heart is not only worn on your sleeve
—It appears on your face, especially in the soul of your eyes.

~M.L. Carmen Forcier ~

The day I left Windsor, my hometown, my parents drove me to the train station; my father seemed upset. As for my mother, she seemed to be crying, saying, "I did not know what I was doing!"

I was so sure of myself back then and so angry with both parents and their comments and feelings did not even come close to touching me!

Alan met me at the train station in downtown Toronto (where we'd first met—we were so happy to see each other!). He drove directly to Scarborough General Hospital, allowing me time to settle in my room in the nurse's residence.

It was near the first of July, 1972, when I began my new life as a student nurse. Every girl in my class went home on weekends as they lived close enough to the school; as for me, I always said I was visiting friends when Friday classes ended. Of course the "friend" was Alan.

Our dates to restaurants every weekend was the greatest thrill! (My parents had taken my sister and I out, once.)

Whether it was a Subway sandwich and a soda for ninety-five cents, or breakfast with bacon and eggs, toast and fresh fruit (so as to minimize the greasy taste of the meal) or a steak burger—which was divine—Alan and I were living a very good life, tremendously enjoying each other's company, feeling the great passion of falling in love!

As the months flew by, he paid for my uniforms, nursing shoes, medical books, etc. and was often generous in paying for some of my groceries. It was near December of 1972 when he was able to make the last payment for all of these necessary items, so close to my upcoming graduation day, March 23, 1973.

★ ★ ★

My mom would write me every week with her faithful duty of criticisms—though no money was ever sent, nor did I ever ask!

★ ★ ★

Alan brought me to meet his mother and family in Maniwaki P. Québec during the fall of 1972. Turned out his name was Albert which at first I thought was a funny joke—but no, this was his REAL name...Ha! What a surprise!

BEING LABELLED... THE STUDIOUS ONE

Seek first to understand, and then you can be understood.

~Steven Covey~

I'd spend all of my time writing and researching, truly loving my class assignments. Meanwhile, back at the ranch, so to speak, all of the other students went out partying, many times with resident doctors—which was absolutely forbidden. They never did get caught!

Being so in love with writing and reading, I was constantly asking questions in the classroom, having been curious all my life! My fellow classmates got to the point of laughing and snickering whenever my hand went up, seeking an answer.

Every two or three months, we would have one-on-one evaluations, given by our teachers, to discuss our progress and answer any questions or concerns we may have. When my turn arrived, I sat across my favourite teacher. Her name was Kathleen. Following her encouraging comments on my behaviour and interest in the course, huge tears ran down my face! She asked what was wrong. Attempting to explain myself, I shared with her my feelings of rejection from the others every time I'd ask a stupid question! She clearly felt how upset I was. Her very words were:

"Carmen...there are no stupid questions! Ignore the laughing...Do not ever stop questioning!"

★ ★ ★

The supervisor found one of my essays so interestingly written that she asked if I would allow her to have the doctors on staff circulate my work for them to read. What an honour! The subject had been researched from the book called *The Prophet* by Kahlil Gibran.

ONE MORNING, MID-JANUARY, 1973…

One sword can rarely overcome a score,
though one heart may be braver than a hundred.

~Samuel James Watson~

One morning, mid-January, 1973, I awoke with very painful knees. As the day drew to a close, they hurt more and more. When class was dismissed, my knees were swollen, red, and hot to touch!

I found myself on the floor after leaving my desk, unable to hold my weight without GREAT PAIN! Among the staff and students, there was some concern. Two people helped me up to my room, saying I was now on bed-rest for at least three days until I consulted a doctor. The only thing I was allowed was to use the washroom!

On the third day, my knees felt better therefore I made the decision to take the bus to the clinic which prescribed me with "the pill," as I wanted to know if this was the cause of all my pain. Being in residence, we the students had to sign out and then back in so that the school knew what time we left and if we honoured our ten pm curfew. The woman hired to be present at this desk would report any information that seemed out of the ordinary. We were all under strict scrutiny.

Signing back in the log book, two hours later, I went straight to my room to resume resting. (By the way, the pill had not been the cause of my flare-ups.)

Not long afterwards, one of my teachers knocked on my door, flabbergasted that I'd left the premises, as I'd had been privileged in not having to attend classes with no permission to leave the room! She asked where I had gone. My reply was that I'd gone to a clinic. Of course she asked, "What kind of clinic?" I decided to let her know that was private information. Whoops! Huge mistake!

The next day, I was brought to Emergency to be examined by a doctor, who determined the inflammation of my knees was caused by a condition called bursitis. Taken back to my room via wheelchair, the orders remained as total bed-rest!

By this time, each student took turns sitting at my bedside for the full length of ten days or so to observe any kind of signs which may indicate something else might be wrong.

On one of those days, a fellow student told me, in confidence, that my teachers suspected I had rheumatic fever, because I'd just gotten over a very bad cold. Seemed I had all the signs pointing in that direction.

Well, to say the least, she scared the s*** out of me! It was finally determined that I was never seriously ill. The day the pain in my knees was gone, I was healthy once again!

THE SUPERVISOR CALLED ME...

Perhaps the greatest social service that can be rendered
by anybody, to the country and mankind, is to bring up a family.

~George Bernard Shaw~

The supervisor called me into her office on several occasions following my so-called unhealthy events, constantly questioning me about my ties with the clinic I'd visited a few weeks previously, and where I was going every weekend. My answers to both her questions were that this was a private matter. She never did get the answer she was digging for! Meanwhile, I was one among many who saw their boyfriends on weekends!

A while later, one of our teachers, who was actually a nun, told me that if all of these incidents had occurred months earlier, I would have been dishonourably discharged from the nursing program! Being as there were less than three months to graduation, I was allowed to finish my studies! What a HUGE relief!

We'd written our final exam in mid-March; when the results came back, Kathleen (the teacher who'd encouraged me to continue questioning) was calling out our names one by one, stating our results in front of the whole class. The passing mark was 320.

She called my name, and upon handing me a slip of paper, her truly encouraging nod towards me was unmistakable! I'd passed the required exam with a 640 point result! WOW! What a day that was!

GRADUATION DAY...

A beaten child's eyes, does not disguise...
the heartache inside...

~M.L. Carmen Forcier~
(Copyright 2002)

Graduation day, set for March 23, 1973, was coming fast. My special friend and cousin Jocy had promised that she and her boyfriend would be there for the ceremony!

Coming in late, I ran to the lockers, and a teacher handed me an orange corsage and said to hurry as everyone was waiting to enter the staged theatre.

While falling in line to the song "We've Only Just Begun" by The Carpenters, my heart beat quickly; the sound was beautiful, inspiring and full of hope. My dream had come true, and there was Jocy, waving to me from her seat. She'd honoured her promise; had she been absent, my day would not have been complete. How I treasured our friendship!

My nursing class took seats on the stage. We were called, one by one, to receive our certificate. To date, this gesture was the most important event of my life.

My parents attended, passing on to me cards of congratulations from their friends. An evening of dining and dancing followed the ceremonies. Later on, I snuck my father up to my room, so proud to show him where I'd lived for the previous ten months!

MYSTIFYING
MOMENTS

ALBERT HAD ASKED ME...

One of the great teachings that I learned in India
is that silence is the only true religion.

~Elizabeth Gilbert~

Albert had asked me to marry him on September 23, 1972. Of course my response was a big YES! We set the date for June 16, 1973. In the meantime, I'd been hired to work at Scarborough Centenary Hospital specialising in sick children.

This facility had been built on a very modern plan. The concept was made to serve the nurses and save time. In one room, we each had six patients; when the need arose, we'd use an intercom system to order either ice for the croupettes or individual meals for the children, and so on.

At that time, I rented a room in their nurse's residence. Our wedding date was fast approaching, so three months later, I handed in my resignation, having been accepted at Toronto's Sick Kids Hospital downtown, closer to where we planned on living.

Two weeks before our special day, we found a beautifully-furnished second-floor apartment in a big home way up on a hill. We were beyond pleased! In order to move in, we took a taxi from Albert's rented room, accompanied by our ten or so boxes. The distance cost was nine dollars.

Albert carried all of the boxes one by one, up the thirty-two steps to the porch which in itself had half a dozen steps, finally reaching the second floor with the last of our belongings.

Meanwhile, like any and all other hospitals, after giving a urine sample, the staff asked for an x-ray of my lungs. By sheer instinct, I said to the nurse that I was almost sure I was pregnant. Waiting for results, the news came back that YES, I was definitely expecting a child! I loved this baby immediately and thanked life for this treasure.

Albert was absolutely thrilled. It was Thursday June 14, two days before our wedding! The baby was due January 31, 1974.

TO GO RE-CAP A LITTLE...

Joy is prayer—Joy is strength—Joy is love—
Joy is a net of love by which you can catch souls.

~Mother Teresa~

The previous Sunday evening, I'd called my parents to make sure that everything was in order for our special day of June 16. Albert and I had agreed to marry in my French-Canadian church in Windsor in order to please my mom. Otherwise, we'd have gone to city hall, as there would have been much less confusion and would have definitely been a simpler process than if we involved the church.

My father answered the phone—long distance charges back then were more than three dollars a minute! He immediately said that we should call the priest as he was refusing to marry us! The wedding had been cancelled! (We'd previously gone to Windsor to meet with this priest whom I'd known in high school.)

There I was, with the assistance of the operator in order to reverse the charges. I recognised his voice, and he clearly said that Father Brunette was out at the moment. I repeated this message to Albert; we were both furious. Had I not called Windsor that evening we would never have known anything about this cancellation!

Albert took the phone, called the priest, wanting a definite explanation for all of this miscommunication!

Father Brunette simply said he'd changed his mind.

Continuing the conversation, Albert explained that he had family from Québec coming for this wedding, and if he (the priest) kept refusing, we were definitely going to sue him personally; after all, I'd made the arrangements, reserving the church the previous January!

When the conversation ended, the priest added that his heart would not be in it.

The following Thursday, after midnight, I took the Greyhound bus from Toronto to Windsor, because it was cheaper than travelling during the day. Upon arriving, there was my father, furious as can be, yelling at me all the way home, saying how very inconvenient this whole wedding business turned out to be. What a nightmare!

In a condescending tone, he repeated how it had cost him $800 for the liquor, never mind the catering…the cake…the flowers…the invitations… (which clearly had not been hand-written). My mother had to call everyone at the last minute, convincing them there would be a wedding after all!

Upon arriving at the house, there was my mother, so furious, saying she had had to decorate three boxes to make it look like a real cake. She nastily complained how busy she was because of me—doing someone's hair, sewing my wedding dress, ordering flowers, making meals in between, and so on.

★ ★ ★

My favourite aunt Lilianne, married to a doctor, living in Chicoutimi 100 miles north of Québec city, had over the years, visited our family in Windsor several times with her small children. A few weeks prior to our wedding, my very own mémé flew to Chicoutimi, remaining there for six weeks.

We, Albert and I, deduced this situation would never have occurred had my mom told them we were definitely getting married June 16.

Neither my aunt nor my grand-mother attended our wedding; the two most important people in my life! I always wondered about this situation.

To my friend Mona-Lee!

*You are the richest woman I know; your heart of gold,
your caring for all, your listening, your wisdom, your strength, your
kindness…You bless everyone!
Now bless yourself, dear child, whom I love so deeply.*

**~M. L. Carmen Forcier~
(Copyright 2003)**

SATURDAY, JUNE 16 ARRIVED...

Picture an ocean of abundance.

~Anthony Robbins~

Saturday, June 16 arrived. I was marrying the love of my life.

It was highly unusual for my parents to ever be late for church, although this day was different. We left a little past four pm—the very hour we'd set to marry. Upon arriving at the church, my father went straight to the priest's little room behind closed doors; it was 20 minutes before he came back to us (we were waiting in the entrance hallway).

Finally, Father Brunette came out of hiding, and so began our wedding at four twenty-five pm. Upon entering the church, it felt like we were at a funeral, the atmosphere being so heavy with sadness.

Once the vows were exchanged, the priest blessed the whole congregation—and simply disappeared behind the curtains, never to be seen again! Had my father paid the priest to marry us while in the back room? Chances are, he more than likely did, out of sheer desperation!

The ceremony was followed by a catered dinner in my parent's basement, where we all sat like sardines. Albert and I never danced, as we'd been seated where it was impossible to move without disturbing the whole set-up. Of course, I had not mentioned to my mom that I really wanted to invite all of my friends, with the thought being that my parents could not afford to have any more guests than already planned.

This, at least, would have given me photos and very fond memories of the loving times I'd shared with my companions for so many years during my teens! I guess it was not meant to be.

Take every stone
The bigots of this world
Cast against you
And use them
To build my church
In this world

And when they seek
To oppress you

And when they try
To destroy you

Rise and rise again and again
Like the Phoenix from the ashes
Until the lambs have become lions
And the rule of darkness is no more

~Maitreya~
Friend of all souls
From the Book of Destiny
(researched on the internet)

GIFTS FROM OUR WEDDING…

Your soul is ONE with every galaxy within all universes.

~ M.L. Carmen Forcier~

Gifts from our wedding also included $365—money for which we were desperate, because upon leaving Toronto we had exactly one single penny to our name! As Albert's mom wanted to visit Niagara Falls, we spent our three days of honeymoon in that area.

When she flew back to Québec, our life as a married couple began. I was now working at Sick Kids Hospital and Albert was taking an upholstery course. Although I was nauseous every morning due to my pregnancy, I continued working for the next three months.

On my last day leaving home, I'd been sick, as usual, even though I took crackers before even lifting my head off my pillow. As I descended the thirty-two steps from the porch to the sidewalk below, I was again sick right on the lawn. This is when I decided I could no longer do this walk to the subway, feeling weak, smelling all the wonderful odours once in the subway—with standing room only!

A few days later, I resigned. What a relief!! From then on, morning sickness was a thing of the past!

My mom had sewn my wedding dress, which cost her twenty dollars; my shoes were thirteen dollars. She'd asked me which pattern I wanted, and if I would like some trimmings on the dress. She chose the material, and I chose a pale blue trimming which went from the top of the dress, flowing on two sides from the waist down.

About one month later, we'd gone to Windsor for a long weekend, and upon seeing my wedding dress in my mother's closet, I said that I would take it home with us. My mom responded by saying, "Well, what are you going to do with it? Anyways, there's no rush. I'll bring it to your place the next time we visit Toronto."

That was OK with me! HAH! YUP—try to guess what I'm going to say next!

When my parents next visited us in Toronto, I asked, "Where is my wedding dress?"

This made my mom FURIOUS! How dare I ask her this question!

Her answer was exactly the following:

"I picked all of the trimming off, one stitch at a time...I certainly was not going to waste this by leaving it on the dress. It cost way too much! So I kept it to use on other clothing. As for the dress itself: I cut it into tiny pieces, then threw it into the garbage!"

Was I surprised? Hmmm! She had such a nasty character! Her harsh words threw me into a trance! Hit me like a bomb! Shocked me and shook me to the very core of my being!

What could I say? I was not even allowed to question her motives, although knowing my parents had cancelled the wedding, and we'd made it take place anyways, this was her response to our getting married. FUCK YOU!

WHEN I WAS EIGHTEEN, I WATCHED SESAME STREET EVERY MORNING...

Every human being has two countries:
his own and France.

~Thomas Jefferson~

During my 1st year of marriage, I watched Sesame Street every morning. Whatever that was about? I'll never know!

I was also a clean freak, having to do housework every day, as I was obsessed with the thought, "What if someone comes to visit? What would people think if my place was not spic-and-span?"

Every day after work, Albert would say, "Did you do the dishes?" and of course I never did do that part of housekeeping—thus every evening, Albert did the dishes before dinner, and afterwards also!

Our budget for groceries was $12.50 per week. Yep! Sometimes we bought a box of cookies, when luck would have it. Other times, we managed to buy a roast beef. On the evenings when I chose to cook this special meal, I would ask Albert if he could he dress in his grey jacket, the one he'd worn at our wedding. And so we celebrated our union this way every so often; it was heaven to be so in love, living in a beautiful place, expecting our first child, giving thanks for the health with which we were all so blessed.

Every once in a while, my parents drove from Windsor to visit with us in Toronto; it was only a few hours drive away. During one of their visits in late July, Albert said, "Carmen is pregnant!".

OH! Boy! Not such a great idea—especially for my mom! AHHHHH! She went straight to our bedroom, slamming the door behind her. Albert followed to comfort her and to assure her that he would always take care of me!

★ ★ ★

Our income was cut by more than half because I had left my job, although we always managed to have ten dollars' worth of subway tokens every two weeks. We were so very happy together, expecting our first child and even being thankful we had a telephone, so tight were our finances.

By the fall, Albert was going to upholstery school and was also working in silk-screening for a friend he'd known for many years! There we were, paying for the course, with Albert making four dollars in two jobs, working all kinds of hours.

★ ★ ★

Christmas was fast approaching AND my aunt Lilianne and uncle, John were driving from Chicoutimi, P. Québec; also, my aunt Sue was coming from California with her two little girls, so we HAD to be in Windsor that year especially!

As I was almost eight months pregnant, my doctors had to grant me permission to travel by bus from our home in Toronto to Windsor! This occasion was one of the happiest of our lives so far.

During our visit, I began suffering from an extreme pain in my upper chest. My uncle John, being a cardiologist, told us not to worry, that this would pass. My mom also called her family doctor, and he also said there was no need for concern! Meanwhile, back at the ranch, I was in so much pain it was interfering with my breathing and my sleep, both afternoons and nights!

One night, my mom convinced me to take "Eno"—the stuff that helps with indigestion. I hesitated because I was on a salt-free diet, and I knew I was risking retaining even more fluid. In the end, I did swallow a glassful, although this never changed the level of my pain.

Several years later, a nurse informed me that even back then, it was clearly known that if a mom had chest pains while pregnant, convulsions were very much a threat to her body!

Once I arrived back in Toronto, my doctors told me that I had protein in my urine, and admitted me immediately to the hospital! Still three weeks away from the expected birth date of January 31, and barely looking pregnant, I had rising blood pressure—all signs of pre-eclampcia indicating I was in danger of either losing the baby or even my own life! As a nurse, I had an inkling that I was in trouble.

AS THE DAYS WENT BY...

I cannot reach everyone
but everyone can reach someone.

~Loretta Long~

As the days went by, my blood pressure was taken often; nurses listened to the baby's heartbeat almost every fifteen minutes or so. I'd been followed closely by two specialists due to my scleroderma and was reassured that the chances my baby would inherit these genes were one in a million; this was most comforting!

A few days later, one of the resident doctors who'd followed my case from the start, along with another called Doctor Warren, came to explain that they would more than likely have to do a C-section. Immediately, my eyes filled with tears and I was inconsolable; I felt extreme fear, resulting in the rise of blood pressure. NOT GOOD at all! They quickly wheeled me into a labour room where I was hooked up to a monitor, permitting the staff to follow my baby's heartbeat. I'd been told to remain very still on my back so as not to interfere with the monitor, though every time I turned to one side or the other, one of the doctors would immediately enter the room asking me if I had moved. My answer was always "Yes' as it was very uncomfortable to lay in one position. By five pm, both residents entered the room, explaining that they needed to do an amniocenteses to locate the baby's placenta.

NOW...YOU HAVE TO TAKE NOTE HERE...

We are exquisite expressions of the cosmos.

~Unknown~

The doctors said the results of the amniocenteses would not be known until the next morning AND I later learned that I "had to" give birth before midnight that evening! They'd told Albert the baby would not live, due to my small abdomen. All alone in the waiting room, he worried himself sick, though no one had given *me* this news; of course I had no doubts at all about the baby's good health. My breathing exercises helped relieve some of the pain from the contractions, which were actually quite bearable.

During the amniocenteses procedure, the doctors used a very, very long needle piercing into my skin, and upon entering the uterus, I'd scream out from extreme pain. They attempted this process three times, and each time ended with the same results.

Following this, one of the residents attempted to break my water. Nothing happened, even after his second attempt! Another little surprise was that if I had to have a "B.M." I was only allowed a bed pan; needless to say, I kept it all inside (smile)!

The time was now nine-thirty pm. Doctor Warren came to my bedside, holding my hand in a very tight fist, saying my name out loud, encouraging me to have this baby NOW! He seemed desperate, and I really felt his panic! All of a sudden, I felt like I had to push—and oh! the pressure was a thousand times that of a B.M. My god, this was powerful stuff! Incredible! The doctor kept telling me to push, push, push, though I insisted giving birth in a sterile environment, meaning the delivery suite!

The six doctors following my case ran for their gowns and masks, quickly moving me to the delivery room. I'd held my baby in for approximately five minutes in total. HIGHLY not recommended! AND how so terribly uncomfortable!

Finally, I was told to push once, and then again. The baby felt like she had flown out of me!

"Could I please see her?" I asked.

After weighing her at three pounds, six ounces, she was enveloped tightly, with most of her face covered. In the wink of an eye, they quickly showed me her half-covered face, and whisked her in an incubator to the nursery, where Albert was able to bond with her.

During this time, the doctor was explaining that part of the placenta was missing; he had to go digging back inside my body! Not having received anything for my labour pains, I begged with all of my heart for him to please give me something for the pain!

The dark mask invading my face with anesthesia put me out until I awoke in my room a short while later.

We named her Chantal Myrielle, and her birth date was January 7, 1974.

DUE TO MY EXTREMELY SORE BEHIND...

Imagination is more important than knowledge.

~Albert Einstein~

Due to my very, very sore behind, it took me almost half an hour to reach to nursery from my hospital room, which most people could travel in a few minutes. The nurses placed a hard wooden stool beside my baby's incubator, saying I could not yet hold her, although I could reach in and feel her. All the while, my motherly emotions kicked in quite heavily; not having held her after birth, I became overwhelmed at the miracle that had come from my body. WOW!

The first thing I noticed were three iodine marks on her left brow. The nurses said I'd have to ask the doctor about it. That same afternoon, Doctor Wallace answered my question by saying that those marks on my baby's left brow had been caused by the amniocenteses!

So stunned was I that I blurted out, "You could have blinded her had she moved!" Now I remembered—the pain from the long needle had not hurt *me*...I'd felt the *baby's* pain instead! OH! Goodness gracious me! I was beyond shocked!

My next question was, "Why am I so darn sore in the vaginal area?" His response was that he'd made the decision to cut me from the vagina to the anus in order to help facilitate the baby's birth; in this way the child had no problem whatsoever coming down through the canal. WELL…what can I say?

For the next eight weeks, I was always in extreme pain, and I was unable to walk normally. I was discharged from the hospital within a week, and Albert and I decided to visit Chantal every second day.

OH BOY! This meant going down to the first floor of our apartment, followed by the porch steps AND the thirty-two steps from the porch to the street EVERY SECOND DAY!

As if this were not enough, we also walked to the nearby subway station, down those fifty steps to reach the underground, THEN sit on the hard seats this transportation offered.

Just when I thought it was not possible to make my pain any worse, I discovered that I was unable to breast-feed Chantal as her mouth was way too small for my nipples! To add to my feelings of failure and distress, the chair I sat on was very hard, adding GREAT PAIN to my bottom!

After our visit to the hospital, we had to trek back in the heavy snow the same way we came-—which of course included all of those steps! We did this FOR EIGHT FULL WEEKS. Please, someone help me!

★   ★   ★

Sitz baths were highly recommended to avoid infection, especially in my case—so I would sit in the bottom of our tub, three times per day, for the required eight weeks. Following these eternally painful duties, the day did come where I could say DONE!

Gratitude unlocks the fullness of life.
It turns what we have into enough, and more.
It turns denial into acceptance, chaos into order
confusion into clarity...
It turns problems into gifts, failures into success,
the unexpected into perfect timing,
and mistakes into important events.
Gratitude makes sense of our past, brings peace for today,
and creates a vision for tomorrow.

~Melodie Beattie~

RECOGNISING
REALITY

WELL…THE WORD DONE…

Memories unfolding flowers…
Flowers unfolding memories.

~M.L.Carmen Forcier~

Well, the word "done" mentioned a page earlier was not exactly what really happened. Actually, I was just at the beginning of my chosen journey of being a good wife and mom. In the first week following the birth of our little Chantal, my mom came to help with the meals, etc. Seven weeks later, Chantal's weight was five pounds, four ounces, and she was finally ready for discharge; my sister came to visit, and we both took her home very carefully.

The next four weeks absolutely whizzed by! Unbelievable! Chantal, being a "preemie" baby, had to be fed every three hours. No need for a clock—she was always on time when hunger hit her! Between making formula every day, and taking turns to feed Chantal every second night with my sister, we became exhausted very quickly!

Her schedule was every three hours: noon, three pm, six pm, nine pm, midnight, three am, six am, nine am, etc. AND, it was an absolute MUST that she burp properly after each feeding. Well, it only took ten minutes to feed her; THEN, there was a patient wait of two and a half hours to finally hear her burp, which meant there was only half an hour before every next feeding! This happened at every feeding—for about four months!

Just before my sister left to go back home to London, Ontario, Chantal awoke one night, screaming and screaming! Gizèle, sleeping in the baby's room, called out my name to come quickly. I ran so fast; there was Chantal's little head, stuck between the wooden bars of her crib! OH! God! What could I do? Instinctively, I forced her head back into the crib, hoping for a miracle! AHH! WHEW! It worked, and she was fine!

Once my sister left to go back to her hometown, I was doing everything by myself. On certain nights, Albert would get up for feedings, though he could not stay up for two and a half hours to burp her. This meant getting about thirty minutes of sleep every three hours—and it was like this every day for the next three months! I absolutely looked like a green tomato, HONESTLY!

Albert was a great support all 'round, especially with the making of the formula. Now, with *moi* being the perfectionist, if Albert dropped one nipple on the floor or even on the kitchen counter, I would always insist that it be boiled for another ten minutes. This was driving him crazy! It took a full year before I started eating, feeling, and looking normal.

★ ★ ★

I had gained thirty-five pounds during the pregnancy; I had no amniotic fluid in my uterus on the night Chantal was born, and when I passed my water, the amount was two thousand ccs, one thousand ccs twice. After measuring my output, the nurse said she'd never seen anyone pee that much in one time. My weight went from 170 pounds to 123 overnight. My stomach was actually now inverted!

★ ★ ★

A short time later, we had her baptised for the love of my mom. At the age of one Chantal weighed only eleven pounds; others can weigh more than this, even at birth.

EVEN THOUGH WE HAD A WATER HEATING SYSTEM…

Remember the ones you've touched and helped grow,
bloom in your heart like a beautiful rose.

~M.L.Carmen Forcier~

Although we had a water heating system, the owners always seemed to have the thermostat on low, because we were often cold during the winter months. One day, Chantal, being about three or four months old, sneezed. That was it! We decided to move so our little one would not catch cold or anything more serious, such as pneumonia.

Finding another apartment was fairly easy, though we needed to put one month's rent down as a damage deposit, which my father was kind enough to cover. Living in this building was very nice—there was a beautiful lounge upon entering the building, as well as washers and dryers and a swimming pool; it was also clean and well-maintained, and we benefitted from a better heating system.

At this time, Albert wanted to take an English writing class held on Monday and Tuesday evenings. We decided that that I'd work night shifts for one year, and I made arrangements with the hospital to have every Monday and Tuesday off, permitting me to watch over Chantal while Albert went to school. Albert would drive me to work for the start of my shift at eleven pm; when mornings came, I'd take one subway and two buses, arriving home around nine am.

★ ★ ★

Luckily, sleeping during the day went well for me. Every morning, I would remind myself with great pleasure that while I slept, most people were going to work. This was a very comforting thought!

NEARING THE END OF THIS ONE YEAR PERIOD…

Failure isn't falling down. It's staying down.

~Devotional Book for Women~

Nearing the end of this one year period on a particular Sunday evening, I began calculating my last day of work. In order for me to be eligible to receive unemployment benefits for a full year, I had to get pregnant that very evening, because I had exactly six more weeks to work, which gave me the exact timing needed to pass a pregnancy blood test before leaving my job.

There I was, begging Albert, repeating that I had to get pregnant that very evening, and no later! Once we made love, I propped my behind up onto several pillows to make sure I would definitely get pregnant (smile). Six weeks later to the day, tests showed I was pregnant for the second time! That Sunday evening mentioned earlier was really and truly the day our second child was conceived. Talk about a close call!

★   ★   ★

Upon giving my resignation, the head supervisor asked me if I wanted them to keep my position open. Believe it or not…YES…this was the way of the world back in those days, where most employees were respected to that extent—of course, having a Union was definitely helpful!

I did start receiving my U.I. Checks within the next few weeks and was entitled to the full one year of benefits! YEAH! We'd succeeded in our mission (smile)!

DURING THIS SECOND PREGNANCY...

Oh child! Never allow your heart to harden.
Welcome the unicorn into your garden.

~Phyllis Gottlieb~

During this second pregnancy, I now had a fully-fledged, graduated gynecologist. Near my fourth month of gestation, I developped pre-eclampsia, which goes hand in hand with high blood pressure, swelling, and possibly seizures if the illness gets really serious. My doctor emphasized that I could not gain more than twenty-five pounds total, which meant that with every monthly visit, I should not have gained more than two or three pounds.

Well, being twenty years old and not really worried about the weight gain, I would eat anything and everything, totally ignoring doctor's orders of being on a low-salt diet. Pizza was my favourite! I would cheat for three weeks then the week before my doctor's appointment, I would eat very sensibly.

Although I was cheating, my weight was going up at the expected pace, until I neared my eighth month; the doctor's scale indicated a weight gain of twelve pounds over a period of four weeks! YIKES!

Upon entering the room, my gynecologist threw my chart onto the bed and was furious! He adamantly said, "Do you want a dead baby?" He was so disgusted with my negligence! The very much-deserved speech I got put me back on track to a healthier lifestyle.

★ ★ ★

Liliane Michelle was born healthy, on November 21, 1975. Her nickname became "Lilo", the name she has always chosen to go by. Her weight was a normal seven pounds, and she was smiling within minutes of being born. Growing up, she was always happy, jumping up and down out of sheer joy, and laughing most of the time. She would become my keeper and care giver when I became ill years later.

ALBERT, HAVING TAKEN A COURSE...

Starting a quarrel is like breaching a dam,
so drop the matter before a dispute breaks out.

~Proverbs 17:14 (NIV)~

Albert, having taken a course to become a computer operator, had increased our income, which also became more secure than in previous jobs. One day, we decided to drive from Toronto to Ottawa in order to leave his résumé at the government of Canada's Taxation Office. Albert had family living near this city, so we thought it would be a good idea to move close to them if we got the chance.

Well, about one week later, the Taxation Office of Ottawa called with the news that they had accepted Albert's application, asking, "Could you start in a month?" Of course the answer was an immediate YES followed by jubilation; he was offered a salary of $11,300 per year! WOW!

Leaving Toronto meant a lot of packing and shipping. Albert and I and our two little ones drove to Ottawa in the moving van, arriving very late on a Friday night. It was also raining cats and dogs...like...a lot!

Marc, his older brother, came to help bring our boxes into the new apartment. It had been understood that Marc would then drive back to Toronto the next day, with Albert, in order to get our car.

Upon their return, Albert accompanied Marc back home; as he was leaving, he said to Marc's wife, "Well, you are welcome to visit any time!" Pauline answered in a very disinterested tone, "OH! We do not go out very often!" BANG!—first rejection!

The next morning, I called Grand-maman (Albert's mom), to ask her if she was happy that we had moved. Her response was, "Well…I feel you are closer." BANG! Second rejection!

This was a HUGE lesson for us to never again move near any family members.

One year later, we moved to Québec city, creating enough distance to lower the pressure of not having been accepted after all the efforts we had made!

The next two years were somewhat difficult, as Québec city is composed of a very closed-in society—meaning, if you are not born there, you are considered a stranger, even though we were both bilingual and very passionate about being a part of our history in this 400-year-old city but BANG! more rejection!

In our first apartment, there occurred a fire that left us devastated as we had no insurance. I'd been quick to save myself and our little ones from burning, although we had inhaled a lot of smoke.

We were able to purchase a semi-detached home by borrowing the $5,000 down-payment from the builder himself; at the same time, tension was rising at Albert's workplace. BANG! Again! I mean, how much can one take?

By April 1, we moved into our very own home. As life would have it, our neighbours on each side did not want to have anything to do with us, because we were outsiders, we had no curtains, no washer and dryer, nor were we even close to their levels of income. A few months later, we found ourselves on unemployment insurance! BANG! That took the whole cake!

Six months later, we lost our house, and moved across Canada to the furthest city on the map—Vancouver, B.C., thousands of miles away from everyone!

PART FOUR

DOMINIC, OUR SON...

Repetition is the mother of all skills.

~Anthony Robbins~

Dominic, our son, was conceived in our beautiful home and born at l'Hôpitale Sacré Coeur in Québec city, August 9, 1979. There were no complications; it was the best pregnancy I'd ever had!

When he was two months old, we sold all of our belongings to a couple who bought all that we owned for $600; this barely got us to Vancouver where Albert had been offered a job as an experienced silk screen printer.

My sister chose to come with us in her small Toyota as we had just gone bankrupt, and our valuable things had gone to cover the costs involved.

So there we were: Dominic sitting in a small portable baby seat in the back with my sister and I on either side. Chantal and Lilo sat together in the passenger seat in the front, with Albert driving, taking turns with my sister. I did not have my license at the time.

We arrived in Vancouver October 29, 1979. Having exhausted all of our funds, we were forced to ask my sister for help. This made her understandably very angry as she had just received a severance package from her former job; she would state that this was her freedom money and felt quite uncomfortable lending us money until we got back on our feet. Also, we all knew we'd never be able to pay her back!

We found a townhouse project near schools and transportation; it was close to Albert's new job, although it took three weeks before we could move in. When the time came, we just fell in love with the place, having been in a cramped motel room for three weeks.

Our newly-rented home had three bedrooms, a kitchen, and a dining and living room. A few days later, my sister's furniture arrived from London, Ontario.

She occupied one of the bedrooms, and the three little ones took the second bedroom. Albert and I shared the master bedroom, which included quite a large closet where our children would often play when Vancouver's rainy seasons were in effect—which occurred quite regularly!

The rest of my sister's furniture filled the dining and living rooms, which was really great, because we had sold all of our belongings. During the next few months, there was quite a lot of tension; we were all adjusting to a new city, being very far from home—plus I was showing signs of paranoia and depression (of which I found out the meaning after being hospitalized six months afterwards).

A few months passed. Coming home from a Sunday drive, we saw the front door to our townhouse wide open, and the inside totally empty. It appears that I had previously asked my sister to leave because it was becoming unbearable, having too many souls living under one roof. She'd arranged with a neighbour to help her move into her new apartment. We did not hear from her for more than six months. There it was again—more rejection!

We'd arrived on a Thursday, and Albert started working the following Monday. He'd been hired as a silk screen printer, although the owner would often have him going on the road as a salesman, selling their product (flags). Turns out he was closing deals left and right without even knowing he had this talent!

The owner finally purchased a car of Albert's choice, which was a 1980 Mustang, allowing him a lot more freedom to find new clients. We simply made the monthly payments.

M. L. CARMEN FORCIER

Now the wife of his employer would often send Albert down to be a silk screen printer every now and then. At one point, while on the road selling again, the girl from the sales department (who'd been on maternity leave for one year) had returned to work. Because Albert was a natural at selling, the owner asked him to fire this woman, as he was to take her place in the sales department. Of course, Albert absolutely refused to do such a thing and thus was sent back down to the silk screening room in the basement.

Knowing no one in this new city, it took time for us to adapt. We enrolled Chantal into kindergarten, and got to know some of her teachers. Most of our neighbours had also moved in, although I was not the kind of person to have known how to make friends since I'd been in high school!

As life would have it, I was feeling very insecure, frightened and always calling Albert at work because I was so overwhelmed by everything! Life was caving in on me real fast, and I would often be desperate for Albert to come home and help me with the children. On one of those occasions, Albert left work to settle some dispute between the children and myself. A half-hour later, one of Albert's fellow employees called to say that he was fired! BANG—rejection once again!

Now in April-May of 1980, my husband started noticing my odd behaviour, and I was also conscious that I was not thinking very clearly. I remember not being able to wipe the dishes because I couldn't decide which side of the plate or bowl I should dry first, or if I should be picking up the knives and forks before the bigger pieces. I was consciously confused, not knowing why.

I also remember thinking I'd made a great discovery about understanding something my husband had written in a manuscript he was planning on having published. He would often refer to the letter X in his writings, as something or other, and I remember saying out loud, in a most excited voice, "I get it, I understand X now—X, Y, Z!"

Of course, the equation in MY mind made perfect sense, but I was no longer in the realm of normalcy, to the great disappointment of my husband! He explained to me that I had to go to the hospital, and because I *knew* that I was not exactly OK, I agreed.

ALBERT CALLED 911...

Never send to know for whom the bell tolls
for it tolls for thee.

~Unknown~

Albert called 911, explaining his emergency—then went to a neighbour's house to ask if the woman could watch over our three children.
Meanwhile, the ambulance arrived while I was alone. The first attendant
looked like the priest who had married us, and the second one looked like
my cousin Richard.

Because of this, I began thinking there was going to be a huge parade
celebration in the streets of Montréal—just for me!—where everyone I'd
ever known, anyone who'd rejected or hurt me in the deepest ways possible, would be witness to the kind and loving person I'd been throughout
my life. I could see in my mind all of those people cheering and waving,
as now they were all my friends and were so sorry I'd had to go through
so much pain. My impression was that I was meant to suffer so that I may
learn the necessary lessons.

This is where I started to become "higher and higher" due to my as-of-
yet-unknown illness—"higher" in the sense of being manic, although not
one person at the hospital knew what was wrong with me!

I laughed at just about any subject and cracked jokes, over and over, and
was full of overflowing happiness, glory and wonder at life as a whole!
Many years later, my psychiatrist explained to me that a Bipolar HIGH

is ten times that of a heroin HIGH! Just imagine in what realm I was living in!

Upon arriving at emergency, one of the female nurses pointed to a door, telling me to wait inside until they were ready to admit me as a patient. Well, as it turned out, I somehow went into the wrong door and found myself surrounded by all kinds of pipes and steam. Not only that, BUT there was a tall man standing there (I now assume was an engineer) looking down on me, caressing my breasts! OH! My! God! I was terrified, knowing clearly that I had to run out of this room ASAP! No kidding, eh?

Finding myself back in the corridor where I'd been upon my arrival, I began running FRANTICALLY towards the doors leading to the outside. My thoughts were that I was in a dangerous place where people were after me, as if I'd committed some crime! WOW! Talk about being scared!

A fairly young male nurse saw me running away and immediately said my name. They'd been looking for me! I was to follow him so that a doctor could assess my mysterious behaviour. There was absolutely no way I was going to follow his instructions after being told to go to the room with the pipes and the tall strange man!

The nurse kept insisting that it was OK to go with him, and that I was safe. A few moments later, I found myself in a prison-like caged room with a mattress on the floor. OH! God!

I was realising that I was not in the best of situations, to say the least. One female nurse asked me to take off my clothes, and to slip into a hospital gown, adding that some doctor would be in to examine me shortly. YA! RIGHT! Like I'm going to undress in front of all of the people waiting in the hallways, either as visitors or patients! I thought they were absolutely out of their minds!

Being a nurse, I knew I was in trouble—but it was the "WHY" question I kept asking myself, and I was terrified to the bones! It seemed unreal, and yet, I was conscious of everything that was going on in my immediate environment.

After what seemed to me like a very long time, a doctor finally came, locking the cell door behind him! I was under lock and key and had no idea why!

My TRIP or HIGH was causing me to think I was going to marry Elvis Presley, but the doctor kept repeating that Elvis had died a few years back, letting me know I was definitely talking sheer nonsense. I mean…imagine my confusion, anger, frustration, fears, questions, the vision I'd had about the parade. There were absolutely no frigging answers!

I WAS ALONE AMONG STRANGERS WITH NO ONE I KNEW NOR TRUSTED!

After what seemed like an eternity, my husband finally arrived accompanied by my sister. WHEW! Now, there was a HUGE relief! Honestly, I'd begun thinking I'd been totally abandoned! I was up shit's creek, alright!

Later on, another female nurse (whose features I still remember) came to my prison-like caged door to ask me once again to remove my clothes, slip into the hospital gown, and sit on the mattress! My response to her was that I was not a monkey or a gorilla anyone need fear, and that I was not there for anyone's amusement, and could I please be spoken to in a humane manner AND be removed from this cage which to me was meant for animals only?

I WAS FURIOUS WITH THIS NURSE! Of course, I was blaming her for my being locked up!

(The monkey and gorilla subject came from how my dad had always said that at my birth, I'd been so so ugly that I'd reminded him of a monkey in a zoo.)

This particular nurse began to cry, holding the bars between her fingers. I felt so guilty because it seemed like I'd broken her heart!

I was experiencing heart palpitations. As soon as my husband realized the situation, and told me to calm down; my heart rate instantly went back to normal.

I sincerely said I was so sorry to this nurse, and started crying myself. Encouraged by my husband and sister, I finally undressed. There were two doctors I'd seen on duty that afternoon, one of them female. At one point, she brought me into her office, asking me many questions, trying with all of her knowledge to diagnose me correctly.

TIME WAS PASSING...

If certain music really turns you on,
and makes your spirit soar—grasp it!

~M.L. Carmen Forcier~

Time was passing—but was it slowly or quickly? Then it seemed as if time stopped when Albert said he had to go home to care for our children, AND my sister said she had to go work the night shift at her hospital.

I COULD NOT BELIEVE MY OWN FAMILY!

I asked, "What about me? I cannot stay alone in this cage by myself! You cannot leave me here all by myself!" I was TERRIFIED to put it mildly! Both of them kept trying to explain that they really had to go, telling me everything would be alright, that I was being taken care of.

OH! My God! This was really happening! I started to feel panic, despair, extreme fear, abandonment, rejection, as well as feeling unloved, confused, disappointed...

Finally, after many repetitive explanations, they both left me alone in this prison-like cage to fend for myself! It was unreal! It seemed like an eternity had passed before I saw the female doctor again. This time she gave me a very strong dose of medication that was supposed to make me fall asleep quite quickly.

My fears were on such a high level, that yes, I felt a little tired, although I remained awake until they transferred me to a different area (at around one-thirty am). The same female doctor could absolutely not understand how I could still be awake after the strong sedatives she'd given me hours before. I was brought to a different department, in a room that was well lit, with a comfortable bed.

Only then did I feel safe enough to let myself fall asleep. Apparently, I was observed very carefully the whole night through.

Upon awakening, a nurse led me to an area where other people (ill like myself) were sitting at a table, eating breakfast. I was famished, having eaten little the day before. There was a radio in the room, and of course they were playing the Beatles, so I decided to turn the volume way up there because for me, the words of the music were being sung to me and only me!

This, we learned later on, was part of my being Bipolar. Everything means something, and it's all coming to you in messages—from the words of the songs or TV programs where you are in a most wonderful ecstatic state of mind!

While the music played loudly, I could really hear the words of how much LOVE I was receiving from the Beatles. Of course, the psychiatric nurses are aware, to some extent, how the brain works when their patients act in these manners due to different mental illnesses.

The first one asked me quietly and politely to turn down the sound, explaining that it was too loud for the other patients.

Here is where the staff becomes very concerned that the patient may get angry, may throw things, hit someone, or even become totally uncontrollable, because at this point, the patient can feel so alone due to the "messages" that are coming through at such a low volume. It made me feel like I'd been cut off from all communications throughout the whole of the universe, because my HIGH was not being fed at the same intensity.

People who live with patients of this sort always have to walk on eggshells so as to not disturb the train of thought in a patient's mind, or have them react to you with vengeance, for whatever reason.

M. L. CARMEN FORCIER

Obsessive-compulsive behaviour also came into play, along with a raging anger which in my case was exacerbated even more—having been raised in fear, anger and hatred.

The following evening, my husband and sister came back to see me. They remained very concerned, as no diagnosis had yet been found! This is when they let me know they'd called my parents (with whom we'd been out of touch for more than four years due to their manipulative mannerisms, control tactics, and their sheer total rejection modes). Our fundamental beliefs were not the exact copy of their own, causing much anger and frustration between all members of our family.

Albert and my sister Gizèle had talked it over and thought that maybe my parents' presence would help me get well again, but I disagreed. Only after being transferred to another hospital—one with better-trained staff and all kinds of activities—did I see my parents.

Their presence depressed me to no end and I was still just as terrified of them both. They had not been there more than a couple of days when Albert and I needed to speak with my one-on-one nurse.

During this confidential session, my nurse told me I'd become ten times worse mentally since my parents had arrived; she emphasized and counselled me by explaining that their visits would have to be monitored and curtailed.

Whenever they did visit, supervision was close at hand…AND as per past experiences (as a child) I would run to the washroom across from the nurse's station and vomit fountains of undigested food from the meals I'd had on those particular days. That's how upsetting my parents were to me!

ON ONE OCCASION...

Without greed
we can feed
All those in need.

~M.L.Carmen Forcier~

On one occasion where my mother was allowed to visit with me, she kept repeating these prayers of hers over and over—although in between her divine lines, she would ask me, "Does Albert beat you?"

I kept saying "No, of course not!"

This happened every day during my parents' visits. As sick as I was, I was consciously losing my mind and therefore knew exactly what my mother was trying to do! If she could get me to admit that Albert beat me, this would have been the great opportunity for both my parents to report this to the nursing staff, so that they could stop Albert's visits and possibly put him in jail for having made me so sick, proving HE was the one who'd made me crazy. My sister also believed this to be true!

Did we feel alienated? Caught in a corner? Scared out of our wits? REJECTED AND STASHED AWAY, MAYBE? My goodness—we were barely swimming above water...and KA-PLOW, there again, my parents were threatening us!

My mother would often walk back and forth in front of the door to my room, repeating, "Just forget all of this and come to Windsor; you can bring the kids and we'll take care of the rest! If you cannot come now…then later, when you're better, we'll send you money for you to take the train with the kids and move to Windsor!"

Did this freak me out? AH! YAH! She was never including Albert while explaining these arrangements and always spoke of these so-called "vacations" when no one else was around!

How's that for being sneaky and filled with bad intentions?

★ ★ ★

Albert was always on time when he came to visit me. At six o'clock sharp, I would see him walk up the hill towards the lounge where I always sat waiting for him. Every single day I could count on him being there for me. I think I would have had conniption fits had he not arrived on any one of those evenings for the full three months while I was in the highly-supervised and intense area of this hospital.

★ ★ ★

My parents had arranged their flight from Windsor to extend to three weeks. They stayed with my sister. One day, the staff decided to give me an evening pass, making it possible for me to have dinner with my whole family at my sister's apartment

Brief note:

During this time, my greatest fear was that Albert was going to cut my legs off on the pool table, located at one end of the hallway of this hospital, where all of us patients walked every day for exercise. I could imagine the blood dripping from the table and how I would then die from hemorrhaging. This, I believe, relates to the fact that I thought people lying in coffins had had their legs cut off…due to the coffin being halfway open.

This is how confused my brain was! It inter-related things from my past, and all of my thoughts became entangled with different events of my life, making me freak out and become so very terrified!

So there we were, enjoying this dinner my mom and sister had prepared. All the while, my dad kept talking about his days in Europe during the second world war and how many soldiers had either lost a leg or two, or an arm, always describing the guts and the blood of it all!

Albert finally asked him to stop speaking on this subject as I feared having my legs cut off back at the hospital. What a sadist my dad was, eh? He knew my fear and fed into it for almost half an hour!

During one of Alberts visits to me—with my parents having been there about ten days or so—he tried to explain to me that my parents came to our home on that very day, asked for our children's clothing, then proceeded to take them away, bringing them to my sister's!

This was kidnapping in the first degree!

We were both so freaked out! We spoke to my nurse about this, although there was really nothing anyone could do, until the full action of taking the children away permanently developed! This I really needed to hear—NOT. Of course it screwed up my brain in the worse possible way!

Albert had known what they were up to...how they wanted to threaten him and more. He gladly gave them the children to take away, knowing all too well my parents were unable to care for three children at their present ages, which were fifty-eight for my mom and sixty-seven for my dad!—not to mention that my dad had never been able to tolerate crying of any sort!

Dominic was six months old when I was first admitted, and from that moment on, for the full six months I was hospitalised, he never once stopped crying, twenty-four hours a day...non-stop, whether it be in his sleep or not! All of the people in the thirty-two townhouses in our project could hear him crying day and night. Some had baby-sat a few times, although after a while they just could not handle his constant cries! And so, the department of welfare was there every evening to care for our children while Albert came to visit me in hospital.

Three days after the so-called kidnapping found my parents returning the children with their belongings, dropping them off like flies. They were quick to drive off without a word. Albert had smiled at them, satisfied at having won our children back safely!

It had now been seven weeks since my admission, and the meds they were giving me had not taken effect, after the usual six weeks when most patients show signs of improvement! I'd been misdiagnosed as being schizophrenic with Manic Depression (Bipolar illness) ruled out. No wonder the drugs I was taking had no healing effects on my brain! DAHH! They were treating the wrong illness! And this for one full year!

My sister and Albert were forever asking my appointed psychiatrist to explain what I was going through and why. He never seemed to give them ANY clear answers. He did not seem interested save for the fact that he was convinced medication did wonders for a patient. PERIOD!

So, after the eighth week went by with still no improvement noticeable in my behaviour, the doctor told me they would more than likely have to give me electric shock treatments. "WHOA!" said I to myself! I'd seen the patients coming from THAT ROOM almost totally unconscious, with their eyes rolling back, unable to walk on their own…some of them sleeping for days!

I was so afraid of this happening to me that, by some miracle, my brain started responding to the meds in a more positive way. And so I was spared from receiving those shock treatments. WHEW!

My stay in that part of the hospital lasted another four weeks, making it a full three months since I'd been admitted.

Now, just before this great accomplishment of mine, my sister approached me and said, "You can come live with me for a while although you'll have get a job eventually to support yourself."

HUH? was my inner reaction. To say that I was stunned does not even come close to describing how I felt. There it was in plain black and white—my sister wanted to break up my family, the same plan my parents wanted to accomplish!

M. L. CARMEN FORCIER

I asked her to leave me alone and told her she would never succeed in taking my family apart nor separate us from each other in any way!

The staff then discussed with Albert that I would be transferred down the hall, to another department where there were occupational activities—group outings to movies, hands-on lessons on how to purchase groceries, etc.

Now once this transfer occurred, I was given the privilege of sleeping at home, as long as Albert brought me back every morning until these treatments ended, lasting another long period of three months.

It was like being in the twilight zone when I'd arrive home, because the colour of the carpet was a fairly orange-y tone which freaked me out, because colours were standing out way too much for me, most likely due to my meds!

I was feeling afraid, uncomfortable, and totally disappointed; I was unable to calm Dominic, and I was also not able to speak to my two little girls due to the fact that I could not make out a sentence, let alone control the weird thoughts and emotions inside my brain!

My parents had come for three weeks (too many). They never once offered any kind of financial assistance, and did not purchase any kind of used kitchen set, or even a chair for the living room. They did not buy any clothes for the children, nor any decent pyjamas or slippers for my long stay in hospital! This did not really shock us; it simply reinforced the fact that they had a few marbles missing and were reiterating their vengeance and hatred towards Albert because we believed in a Conscious Universal Source and not in my mother's god!

★ ★ ★

The evening, my dad was allowed to have one last visit with me; I was sitting up in bed, with my dad in a chair at the foot of this piece of furniture. After talking for a while, out of the very BLUE, he says:

"You know…if I sat up with you in your bed right now…we would look like a married couple."

OH! My God!

Frightened out of my wits, and terrified to leave the room for fear he would stop and touch me sexually—all this and more was going through my head. I ever so slowly slipped towards the door. Luckily, I was still right across from the nurse's station. I begged the staff to please ask the man in my room to leave immediately! I was exasperated!

Fourteen years passed before I saw my father again, in 1994!!

DURING THOSE LAST THREE MONTHS...

It's not the load that breaks you down.
It's the way you carry it.

~Lena Horne~

During those last three months, I would often beg the nursing staff to release me as a patient and send me home where I would rest more comfortably. Of course, the answer was always a great big "No," with them explaining that I needed to stay to let time and the meds take over, hopefully healing me before the three months were over.

Well, that length of time did pass and I was not even anywhere near feeling better. They then had to discharge me anyways, as our medical plan covered patients for a certain amount of time whether patients were healed or not.

The day before leaving, the only plan I had was to vacuum forty-five minutes a day, as we had no furniture and there was really nothing I could do. Albert had to take one full year off work otherwise I would have really lost my mind!

I was not able to sit still for more than five minutes at a time (due to the meds that were making me really jittery) so Albert would take me for long walks. Our two little girls were safe in our townhouse complex with others to play with while other parents watched over them.

As for our poor little Dominic, who still had not stopped crying after my six-month stay in hospital: a woman from social services would often be there, giving Albert and I the freedom to walk in order to help me feel less antsy. It really was an awful feeling, and that constant movement of the body was the only way to help relieve these feelings for very short periods of time.

I would be so relieved when it came time for my rest in the afternoons. AHHHH! Peace at last! Albert cooked all of the meals, bathed the children, walked Chantal to and from kindergarten, while I would remain at home, totally freaked out. He dressed the kids and also raised them on his own, as I had problems expressing myself verbally and was constantly wanting to sleep, likely due to the drugs given me for schizophrenia while I really had Bipolar One illness! Talk about a messed-up brain!

Once that year passed, Albert felt I was somewhat able to be alone —NOT. He also really had to start bringing home more money because, let me tell you, living on welfare is no picnic...no matter what anyone says!

We'd been MOST fortunate that our townhouse project had been built to help families, like ourselves. Therefore, our rent was re-adjusted according to our income for the full year Albert was home to help me cope, even though I was not coping at all!

★ ★ ★

Before leaving for work, he'd make Dominic's lunch, place a few diapers near me on the sofa, set up the "light-bright" game for Dominic to play with, and wound a clock to ring when it was time for me to feed Dominic. He would then leave for the day—but being without him terrified me to no end!

I could hardly stay awake because I was so darn drugged! Dominic was such a sweetheart, because every day for a year or more, he would sit on the floor near me, playing with the "light-bright" without ever crying or running around! He would sit there forever! By then he was eighteen months old, and it's as if he knew I was ill and took care of me by staying by my side. Also, he had missed me so much during my six-month stay in

M. L. CARMEN FORCIER

hospital that I suppose he was beyond relief. In his quietness, he may have felt that I would not go away again if he were on his best behaviour always!

HAVING A FULL-TIME JOB…

*If I've seen further than others, it is because
I have stood on the shoulders of giants.*

~Sir Isaac Newton~

Having a full-time job, Albert continued taking care of everything (as mentioned above) including housework, laundry, etc. A few years later, the children helped with the dishes and light housework. When Chantal was ten years of age, Lilo eight, and Dominic four, they were able to get a paper route. Within the next month or so, they were delivering three paper routes with our help, after school. We lived in a neighbourhood of old houses therefore they had the never-ending task of climbing and coming back down all those stairs. This went on for about six years; then Dominic, aged ten, was appointed sub-manager of a route near our home, where some of the wealthiest people of Vancouver lived. He would take care of the whole route on his own, although when it rained, we would help him with the car, to carry his loads. When the holidays arrived, Dominic would knock on each of his customers' doors; most people were giving him twenty-dollar bills because they were so satisfied with his services, which also included collecting money every month!

Altogether our kids made approx. one hundred and fifty dollars a month for five or six years. This allowed us to live in a very safe area of town, with transportation at our fingertips, and permitted our children to attend some of the best schools in the lower mainland—and went towards their clothing, school supplies, and everyday shoes, including those for gym classes, etc.

In their teens, they took on full-time jobs at the fish and chip stands at the beach near our home. As time passed, they worked part-time jobs until they graduated!

OUR CHILDREN GREW UP…

And I have to say,
that I have great respect for the kinds of people
who are able to recycle their anger and put it to different uses.

~Sydney Poitier~

Our children grew up seeing their dad as a great role model, whom they could see was keeping the family from falling apart due to the fact that I was so ill, angry, obsessive-compulsive, and always afraid of nothing, really—just afraid! I was constantly filled with anxiety which affected anything I attempted to do, filling me with such great fears, I could barely do anything to help around the house! Also, I slept an awful lot, first due to the meds, and secondly, it allowed me to forget I was alive!

As for how they saw me? They grew up with a "pissed-off" mom who did very little to help around the house as I could not do anything!!

We were most fortunate to live in a townhouse project where there were lots of children for them to play with. This helped alleviate much of my anxiety, as they were mostly outside and I knew they were safe!

The only thing I remember teaching them was, for example; when they'd come in whining and crying and hurting from the cruel words the other children were calling them, the only words I could think of in all of those years I was ill were, "If someone hurts you or laughs at you…do not be stupid back, because if you do, then you're just as stupid as they are!" These are the only words I recall saying to help raise our children to become decent citizens!

NOW, BEING BIPOLAR...

Would you light a candle for me, become one with the flame and send me some courage?

~M.L. Carmen Forcier~
(written to my cousin Jocelyne when I felt desperate)

Now, being bipolar makes it very hard to cope with simple daily tasks. I'd acquired a speech impediment, meaning I could not get the right words to speak; my thoughts were constantly jumbled and not even clear to myself. I was obsessed with having the house clean at all times, and was *oh* so angry, twenty-four-seven!

And so my children grew up, unable to express their fears or ask questions. Remembering my anger at dinnertime especially, they would all run upstairs after their meal and stay there until Albert went to explain to them, "Mommy is sick and we have to love her just the same...now go back downstairs and do the dishes."

This went on for years! Every day was the same, repeating itself like a bad nightmare from which I could not wake up! Even my beautiful handwriting was gone, because the messages from my brain to my hand did not make the connection, and so it looked like "chicken scratch" I kid you not!

When I was first diagnosed, a very important part of my treatment was missing—the one where my GP should have immediately recommended me to a psychiatrist!

Thus, for three full years, not one professional in this field of medicine was following either my progress or my regressions!

★ ★ ★

We'd arrived in Vancouver from Québec City on October 29, 1979. From May of 1980 to October of the same year, I spent those long six months in hospital.

As the year went by, I was referred to an inexperienced psychiatrist working in a clinic, who was extremely indifferent to me in all possible ways; for one full year I kept expressing my feelings of wanting to commit suicide on every single visit, every two weeks *for one full year!* She would simply say, "Oh! Just come back for your next visit," not even asking me any questions—nothing! Absolutely nothing!

During these visits, a social worker named Tom was always there to support me in any way he could! He would constantly remind me to call him if I needed anything or was feeling very sick or desperate! One day, I finally did call him! The date was April 29, 1981—which happened to be my mother's sixtieth birthday. This info was nowhere in my mind at this extremely critical time!

You have to remember that yes, my mind wanted me to commit suicide, though my heart did not want to hurt my husband…especially my little ones! This was a HUGE dilemma, almost impossible to deal with—especially the way my brain was NOT working!

I was so, so, *so* depressed that I could no longer stand this deep deep depth or level of extreme pain and GREAT DESPAIR, along with a sense of total loss at not being understood, feeling very, very much alone! No one seemed to know how desperate I really was, and how terrifying these thoughts were to me!

LILO WAS CLOSE TO BEING…

Real friends are those who, when you've made a fool of
yourself, do not feel you've done a permanent job.

~Devotional Book for Women~

Lilo was close to being five years of age, and Dominic was almost two. Chantal was not yet home from kindergarten on the blackest day of my whole life.

I'd finally given up my will to live. It was just more than anyone could ever handle. As much as I felt that I would be hurting my family so very deeply by leaving my kids motherless and my husband devastated, I still went to the cupboard in the kitchen where there was a three-month supply of medication to help treat my misdiagnosed schizophrenia. This meant that all of my meds were not for Bipolar illness!

There were at least five or six different kinds…some for depression, others to prevent HIGHS or anxiety or panic attacks; others were anti-psychotics, just to make sure I would not lose my mind once again…AND the prescriptions had just been filled, meaning the pill containers were almost full for the next three months.

One bottle after another I'd spill in my hand, taking at least thirty tablets in one swallow…and I kept going until I'd taken in six containers of hundreds of pills!

NOTE:

The chalky taste in my throat remained for the next ten years, whenever I took any kind of pill.

Straight away, I called Tom, the social worker; all I said was my name; he was at my home within about ten minutes.

The main reason I'd called him is because I did not want my children to be left alone once I'd passed away; nor did I want them to witness those last moments before my soul left my body.

AS TOM SPOKE TO ME...

Some people complain
because the universe put thorns on roses,
while others praise the universe
for putting roses among thorns.

~Devotional Book for Women~

As Tom spoke to me, I remained very calm, never uttering a single word in regards to what I'd just done to myself. I truly wanted the freaky, terrifying nightmare to end. Every few minutes, I'd run to the kitchen to see what time it was, because as time passed, I felt absolutely nothing. At first it had been fifteen minutes, then thirty minutes, and by the time forty-five minutes had passed, I began to feel somewhat woozy. I knew I was really going to die in the next few minutes!

All of a sudden, this really frightening feeling came over me, realizing I was going somewhere out into the cosmos, alone, imagining my children crying over my body, leaving Tom confused and heartbroken, to have to tell my husband I was no longer among them!

So I hurriedly explained to Tom what I'd done. He asked, "Where are your med bottles?"

After giving him this info, all I remember is hearing and seeing Tom on the phone calling 911. I passed out right then and there...TOTALLY WIPED OUT!

When I came to and became slightly conscious, I found myself in a hospital bed, having a huge urge to pass my water, although I was way too sleepy and way too weak to do this on my own. A nurse helped me up several times. Apparently I was unconscious for three full twenty-four hour days!

WHEN I FINALLY FULLY WOKE UP...

Beware lest your footprints on the sand of time
leave only the marks of a heel.

~Devotional Book for Women~

When I finally fully woke up, doctor's orders meant I was to stay in hospital for two full weeks; this was something I did not quite understand, because I no longer felt depressed; I had an attitude of "What's the big deal? I feel just fine, really—finally!"

The first morning I was presentable, a certain Doctor Robinson walked into my room and asked if I would allow students to ask me questions and observe my behaviour.

Of course, by all means! I thought. *Let me get some attention here!* (This was me just being myself—Bipolar—eternally seeking all of the attention I can grasp!)

The hospital curtain opened to reveal at least ten student doctors. WOW! My mind said, *Hello...welcome!*

Following this, Dr. Robinson sat down with me and asked, "So tell me about your parents."

I looked at him with disbelief and responded by saying. "Do you a few months to hear the story of my life?"

Then I asked him if he was going to follow up with me and become my psychiatrist. His answer was a flat NO, as his patient load was already too much to handle, although he mentioned that his team of interns would put their minds together to find a correct diagnosis.

Upon my return home, I learned that my little Lilo, @ four and a half years of age, had watched firemen pump my stomach—something she never forgot! Someone later on mentioned that you only have about one hour to live if you've swallowed that many pills. By the time the firemen arrived, the clock showed five minutes left before my final hour!

★　★　★

Three weeks later, I was called in to see a Dr. Michael, from Dr. Robinson's team. Arriving in his office with much anticipation, the team had concluded that I indeed had Bipolar One illness. My only response was, "Now please give me the proper medication!"

It was May, 1981 when I began taking Lithium, which was at that time the best medication on the market for this illness.

My GP filled out a new prescription of this med whenever I ran out, though I was not receiving any kind of therapy!

★　★　★

I'd been on stelazine, plus many other meds to treat schizophrenia—not Bipolar illness. It was no wonder I attempted suicide…I'd been royally fucked up! No kidding, eh?

THREE LONG YEARS LATER, IN DR. HENRY BALLON'S OFFICE…

Vision---memory projected into motion.

~M.L. Carmen Forcier~

Three long years later, in Dr. Henry Ballon's office, my internist, who followed up on me regularly due to my scleroderma, looked on as I cried and cried for a good half hour, unable to stop to express the words I so wanted to say, because my brain was so screwed up, unable to shut down the flow of tears.

I learned later that this was a big sign of depression—yet no one recognised this. There was a lack of info on mental illnesses PLUS I did not know what feeling like that meant; I'd felt depressed all of my life, not knowing the difference between feeling sad or glad!

While seeing me like this, Dr.Ballon asked me if there was anyone in particular I would like to see. I said "Dr. Atkinson" whom Ballon knew well. His secretary made an appointment for me to see this doctor-friend of Ballon's, which was three days later, not nine months, which is the usual wait to see a specialist.

Upon entering Dr. Robinson's office, we both recognised each other! He followed me up for twenty years thereafter. Although he'd mentioned that I was his only bipolar patient, he was always on his toes whenever I did get sick, right there on the spot upon my arrivals to emergency on more than one occasion, of course!

★ ★ ★

For the next quarter century, my Bipolar illness never really stabilized my up and down emotions, which went on and on and on! PLUS, Lithium (the medication) causes one to become very, very thirsty! From 1981 to 1996—a period of fifteen years—my intake of water per day was forty-eight cups of fluids, every twenty-four hours! And YES my body gained a lot of weight! I went from 136 pounds to 213 pounds during the next five years or so. That was Lithium's biggest drawback!

A POET'S PRIDE

*One of my close friends recently spoke to me in regards to
my expressed thoughts which she identifies as being...*

...my sanctuary of justifiable indignation

~Wally Lamb~

★ ★

*You don't need organized religion to connect
with the universe. Often a church is the only
place you can go, to find peace and quiet
but it shouldn't be confused with connecting
with one's spirit.*

~Alice Walker~

★ ★

IMAGINE IF WE –
THOUGHT LIKE A TREE…
Trees stand proud,
In our sacred ground
Filtering toxins
Then giving oxygen

Gentle breezes they come,
To dance with the sun
Causing branches to sway
In a harmonious way

Through storms they do weather

Due to Mother Nature,
Their roots of nutrients
Continue their nourishment

From each other they feed
With riveting speed
Not one excluded
All are included

This flow of love,
That rushes and floods
Our beautiful woods
We must heed to because

Imagine if we,
Thought like a tree
Could stand just as proud
Feeding the crowds

Of millions hungry,
On our planet today!

For this to occur,
Our faith must conquer

M. L. CARMEN FORCIER

Override the power
Which neglects this hunger

Now please close your eyes
Feel your heart realize
You are you-man
And I am you-man
No hu-mans excluded

All hu-mans included,

With divinity's strong bond
From within and beyond
We have imaginations
Of eternal horizons.

~M. L. Carmen Forcier~
Copyright 2004

PS

My dad always said in regards to corresponding, living so far away from each other: "Do not forget to write"

AMEN!

CPSIA information can be obtained at www.ICGtesting.com
Printed in the USA
LVOW07s0021090615

441631LV00002B/665/P

9 781460 231241